CREATIVE**ARPEGGIO** **PHRASING**FOR**GUITAR**

Master Arpeggio Substitutions, Scale Sequences, & Chromatic Techniques With Greg Howe

GREG**HOWE**

FUNDAMENTAL**CHANGES**

Creative Arpeggio Phrasing for Guitar

Master Arpeggio Substitutions, Scale Sequences, & Chromatic Techniques With Greg Howe

ISBN: 978-1-78933-472-2

Published by **www.fundamental-changes.com**

Copyright © 2025 Fundamental Changes Ltd.

By Greg Howe, Joseph Alexander & Tim Pettingale

For over 350 free guitar lessons with videos check out:

www.fundamental-changes.com

Join our free Facebook Community of Cool Musicians

www.facebook.com/groups/fundamentalguitar

Tag us for a share on Instagram: **FundamentalChanges**

Cover Image Copyright: Author photo, used by permission

Contents

About the Authors 4

Introduction 6

Get the Audio 7

Chapter One: Introducing Superimposed Arpeggios 8

Chapter Two: Greg Howe Scale Shapes 30

Chapter Three: Designing Ascending Lines 40

Chapter Four: Designing Descending Lines 54

Chapter Five: Chromatic Ideas and Other Shapes 60

Chapter Six: Rhythm & Phrasing 72

Chapter Seven: Cross-rhythmic Motifs 78

Chapter Eight: Performance Breakdown..89

Conclusion 98

About the Authors

Greg Howe

Greg Howe is widely regarded as one of the most innovative and influential electric guitarists of the modern era. Blending rock, fusion, funk, and jazz with technical command and rhythmic sophistication, his playing has shaped the vocabulary of countless players across multiple generations. Since his explosive debut on Shrapnel Records in 1988, Greg has consistently pushed the boundaries of guitar, earning a reputation for both virtuosity and musical depth.

In addition to his acclaimed solo albums, Greg's session and touring credits span some of the biggest names in the music industry. He has performed or recorded with Michael Jackson, Justin Timberlake, Enrique Iglesias, and Rihanna among others, bringing his unmistakable style to arenas around the world. These high-profile gigs speak not only to his technical skill, but to his musical versatility and the respect he commands from fellow professionals.

Greg's importance lies in his unique blend of harmonic sophistication, rhythmic complexity, and melodic phrasing. While many players chase speed, Greg's approach has always been rooted in expression and groove. His superimposed arpeggios, inventive scale shapes and phrasing ideas have become part of the modern fusion playbook, influencing everyone from progressive metal guitarists to jazz-funk improvisers.

Beyond performance, Greg is also a passionate educator. His clinics, masterclasses, and instructional materials have helped thousands of guitarists unlock new dimensions in their playing. He has a gift for breaking down advanced concepts into usable, musical tools – something this book showcases in depth.

Greg continues to tour, record, and collaborate with artists across genres, always evolving while staying true to his voice. Whether on a major stage or deep in the studio, his playing is a masterclass in musicality, creativity, and control. For serious guitarists, his work remains essential study.

Joseph Alexander

Joseph Alexander is one of the world's most prolific and respected music education authors and publishers. As the founder of Fundamental Changes, he has transformed how musicians learn, offering clear, structured, and accessible books that have sold over two million copies worldwide. His work spans genres and instruments, but his focus has always been on helping players bridge the gap between theory and practical application.

A lifelong guitarist and educator, Joseph began writing instructional material after years of teaching privately and encountering the same frustrations among students: confusing theory, disconnected exercises, and a lack of musical context. Their clarity and effectiveness quickly gained attention. Within a few years, Fundamental Changes had grown into a global platform, with a catalogue covering everything from blues and jazz to metal and classical guitar.

Joseph has collaborated with some of the most respected musicians and educators in the world, including Martin Taylor, Josh Smith, Robben Ford, Mike Stern and Trivium's Matt Heafy, and is now honored to be working with Greg Howe on this project.

His ability to shape dense musical concepts into structured, digestible books has made him a trusted name in music education. Fundamental Changes titles are now used by teachers, schools, and players in over 100 countries.

As a publisher, Joseph is known for putting musicians first. His company has opened doors for dozens of authors to share their ideas in a supportive and professional environment, helping them reach a global audience without compromise. Whether writing his own material or producing the work of others, his goal is the same: to make high-quality music education available to everyone.

Introduction

To sum it up in one sentence, this book is about learning to play cooler notes when you're soloing. Have you ever listened to your favorite guitar players and thought, "Wow, how do they put together those amazing melodic lines?" The answer to that question might be much simpler than you think.

In this book we're going to take a deep dive into the concepts that have shaped my playing over the years, and I'll share with you some simple (yet incredibly powerful) guitar hacks I've learned which, when applied, will immediately help your solos to stand out from the ordinary.

You'll almost instantly sound much more deliberate with your note selection, and listeners will be left with the assumption that you're thinking in a more sophisticated manner than most players, even when you aren't. The best part is that you won't need to dig into advanced theory and harmony concepts to achieve this – I've already done a large portion of that work for you.

Throughout this book, you'll find that you're able to apply concepts effectively even before you thoroughly understand them. I say this with confidence because I've been teaching guitar for over 30 years, and during that time have witnessed hundreds of students quickly and successfully apply these hacks – often before the lesson has ended.

These concepts are fun and easy to apply, and if there's one thing I know for sure, it's that the more fun you have during your practice sessions, the more time you'll spend with your guitar; and the more time you spend with your instrument, the quicker you'll elevate your playing to new levels.

The concept at the heart of this book

Here is the premise for the lessons that follow: as a soloist, the majority of my language comes from creating melodic ideas based around arpeggios.

Many people take that to mean if I'm soloing over an A minor groove, I'll be playing an A minor arpeggio of some sort, such as Am7. But, in fact, that would be my least favorite arpeggio to use in that scenario.

The reason for that is the reason this book exists!

When I'm soloing on an A minor vamp, you're much more likely to hear me play Em7, GMaj7, CMaj7 or F#m7b5 arpeggios.

This book will explain why those melodic choices (and more) exist, and how to use them to build sophisticated lines. I'll teach you how I arrange these arpeggios on the fretboard in order to access these advanced sounds. Very quickly you'll come to understand that they are just musical *structures* (like the minor pentatonic scale) that you can use as "scaffolding" to support the scalic language in your solos.

When I first discovered the guitar hacks in this book, my playing improved dramatically in an instant. Now it's time to pass these ideas on to you – with minimal theory, no gatekeeping, and instant usability in your music.

I trust you'll find this to be an inspiring and rewarding and journey.

Greg

Get the Audio

The audio files for this book are available to download for free from **www.fundamental-changes.com.** The link is in the top right-hand corner. Click on the "Guitar" link then simply select this book title from the drop-down menu and follow the instructions to get the audio.

We recommend that you download the files directly to your computer (not to your tablet or phone) and extract them there before adding them to your media library. If you encounter any difficulty, we provide technical support within 24 hours via the contact form.

For over 350 free guitar lessons with videos check out:

www.fundamental-changes.com

Join our free Facebook Community of Cool Musicians

www.facebook.com/groups/fundamentalguitar

Tag us for a share on Instagram: **FundamentalChanges**

Chapter One: Introducing Superimposed Arpeggios

This chapter is going to take you on a short journey that will probably change your whole approach to soloing and composing on guitar. I'll elaborate on the ideas I hinted at in the introduction and show you how you can use *superimposed* arpeggios to create rich, considered colors in your solos.

First, I need to teach you the arpeggio shapes I use, because these fingerings form the backbone of my sound and are an essential element of my style. The good news is, there are only four main arpeggio shapes to learn:

- Major 7

- Minor 7

- Dominant 7

- Minor 7 flat 5 (also known as half-diminished)

I arrange almost every arpeggio I play in a consistent way across the strings. I nearly always place the root note of the arpeggio on the fifth string and play,

- **Two** notes on the fifth string

- **One** note on the fourth

- **Two** notes on the third

- **One** note on the second

- **Two** notes on the first

This 2 1 2 1 2 pattern is a consistent and reliable way to arrange any arpeggio on guitar. (Sometimes I add an extra note at the top of the shape on the first string, just to gain a bit of musical range).

As well as being an efficient and easy-to-remember way of fingering an arpeggio, this pattern forms a framework to my playing, around which I can add scale notes or chromatic *outside* notes to build cool licks – something we'll work on in a later chapter.

In particular, the two notes on the third string often act as a jumping off point, from which I can move smoothly between arpeggio and scale shapes that transition up or down the neck.

Below are the four shapes I use. Learn them thoroughly as you're going to be working with them a lot and they may well become the backbone of your playing too.

The numbers in the circles show which fingers I use to best allow me to shift around the fretboard quickly and easily. They might feel a little unusual at first, but you'll soon get used to them. In later chapters, a lot of the licks and ideas are based around these fingerings, so I recommend you use them if you can.

We'll play each arpeggio from an E root note, so you can clearly visualize and compare the shapes.

NB: when I extend the range of an arpeggio by adding a note (like at the beginning of bar four, where I add the root note to the shape at the 12th fret), I usually play that note with my pinkie and a quick position shift. I've worked quite hard on making it sound as though I'm not changing position!

I use my pinkie in this way to eliminate the hand stretch that would be required if I were to play that note with my third finger. Of course, the higher up on the fretboard you are, the easier it becomes to use the third finger instead, if you prefer. But it's essential to use the "pinkie shift" in the lower regions of the neck to avoid putting stress on your fretting hand.

In this zone of the neck, this Em7 shape could be played either way, but I've chosen to notate it as a pinkie shift, because that's how I play the majority of the time.

Example 1a – Em7 shape

Example 1b – Emaj7 shape

The dominant 7 shape in this zone of the neck is one where I would use fingers 1, 3 and 4 to add the extra note to the arpeggio.

Example 1c – E7 shape

For the minor 7b5 shape, we're back to the pinkie shift, which in this shape demands greater fretting and position shifting accuracy.

Example 1d – Em7b5 shape

Your first task is to practice and memorize these four arpeggio fingerings until they are second nature to you. Work with a metronome and play them cleanly and evenly. Aiming to play them smoothly in 1/16th notes at 100 beats per minute (bpm) is a useful goal. When you've got these arpeggio shapes down, we can move onto the fun musical stuff.

Superimposing arpeggios to create new sounds

This book is designed to teach you my simple method of superimposing one tonality on top of another to create expanded, richer sounds.

So, what does that mean? Essentially, it's about bringing together two things you already know to create something new.

Let's say I play an Am7 chord low down on the neck, while you simultaneously play an Em7 chord in the high register. The result of layering the notes of Em7 on top of Am7 is new, richer color. For the theory-heads, we've created the sound of an Am11 chord.

Let's audition that sound now. I can't stress enough the importance of you *hearing* how this sounds, so if you've not done so already, head to www.fundamental-changes.com now to download your audio and backing tracks.

In Example 1e you'll hear me playing a high Em7 over an A minor groove. What do you think of this sound? I think you'll agree it's more interesting than if I just played Am7 over Am7!

Example 1e

Take a moment to reflect on how you feel about that sound and react to its color. Do you like it? Does it paint any pictures in your mind?

Because arpeggios are simply the notes of a chord played one at a time, we can also play an Em7 *arpeggio* over an Am7 groove to introduce this color into our solos. Example 1f is a *melodic* version of the previous example.

Example 1f

But it's not just Em7 we can superimpose over Am7 – there are plenty of different colors we can use. I said in the introduction that playing an Am7 arpeggio over an Am7 chord is one of my least favorite choices. You're more likely to hear me use an Em7, Cmaj7, F#m7b5 or GMaj7 arpeggio (one of my personal favorites).

In a moment I'll explain why these arpeggios are options and where they come from. Before we get to that, however, I want to show you straight away how I would use this idea in a solo.

I think you'll agree that playing Em7 over Am7 creates a pretty good sound, but of course it's boring to just play up and down an arpeggio shape in a solo. What we need is to integrate that sound into a solo with some other musical ideas.

To get this superimposition idea into a short solo, I'm going to surround it with more standard, "safe" A Minor Pentatonic ideas, and transition into and out of the Em7 arpeggio. I won't go crazy with soloing ideas, so you should be able to clearly hear the Em7 arpeggio notes and how they become the skeleton framework for the melody.

It's important to note that, at a particular point in the solo, I'm *thinking* of the Em7 arpeggio shape and not about Am7 or A Minor Pentatonic, so that I naturally begin targeting those colorful Em7 notes in my solo.

Example 1g

You may have noticed a couple of non-Em7 arpeggio notes in the previous example, but the idea I want you to absorb is that the gravity of the line is *targeting* the notes of Em7 and not the underlying Am7 chord.

Here's a quick hack to remember how to locate the Em7 arpeggio when playing over Am7. You'll be very familiar with the first A Minor Pentatonic box shape at the fifth fret. Just place your finger on the 5th fret, fifth string, within that box shape, then slide up to the 7th fret to launch the Em7 arpeggio. That's all there is to it. Once you know this simple movement to move from one shape to the other, the new sound is instantly under your fingers.

Diagram 1

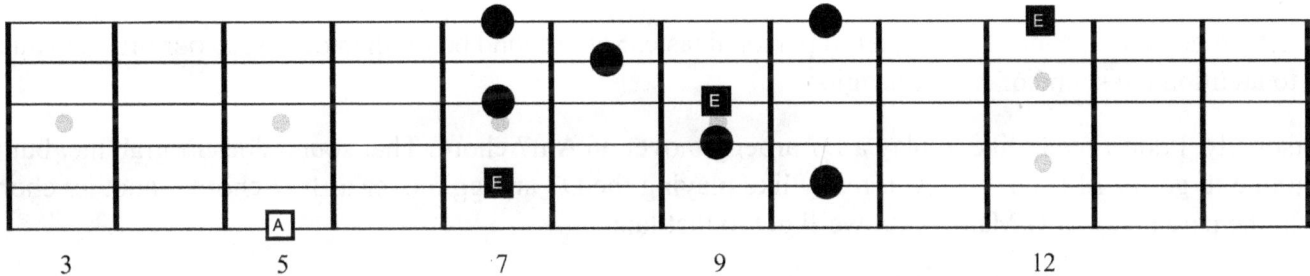

This arpeggio shape can now become the scaffolding of your playing in A minor. Later, we'll learn to add scales, patterns and chromatic notes around this structure, and you'll begin to create powerful licks based around new, richer target notes.

13

Other Arpeggios Superimpositions

You can go deeper into the theory behind this concept later if you need to, but for now I'm going to assume you have a decent understanding of where scales, chords and arpeggios come from.

As a very quick overview, we build chords by stacking the notes of a scale in thirds. This is called *harmonizing* the scale. Applying this process to a G Major scale (G A B C D E F#) results in the follow set of chords:

Scale Tone	G	A	B	C	D	E	F#
Chord/Arpeggio	GMaj7	Am7	Bm7	CMaj7	D7	Em7	F#m7b5

We already know that an Em7 arpeggio sounds cool over an Am7 chord. Look at the table above and you'll see that both chords exist inside the parent key of G Major.

So, here's your next guitar life hack:

*You can play an arpeggio built on **any** note of a parent scale over **any other** chord in that key.*

This is why it works to play Em7, GMaj7, or any other arpeggio from the key of G Major, over an Am7 groove.

Which arpeggios we choose is a matter of personal taste. Some sound better than others, so our first step must be to audition the sound of each arpeggio.

Personally, I don't really like to play a D7 arpeggio over an Am7 chord. That sound doesn't grab me, but if you like it, go for it! (I do, however, really like playing the D7 arpeggio over a Bm7 chord – another chord from the parent key of G Major – but we'll get to that later).

To audition an arpeggio substitution, record yourself playing the chord/groove you want to play over. Then play a high voicing of the chord you want to superimpose. If that chord sounds good on top of the other, then it'll work great as an arpeggio when you solo.

Tip: the arpeggios that work best are the ones built from the notes of the original chord. Am7 contains the notes A, C, E and G. So a great starting point is to explore the sounds of Am7, Cmaj7, Em7 and GMaj7.

But this is not a hard and fast rule, because an F#m7b5 arpeggio sounds great over Am7, for example. Let your ears be the judge.

When you realize that any arpeggio in the *parent key* is available to play over any chord in the key, interesting things start to happen. Look at the table again and you'll see that there are three minor arpeggios you can play over any chord, and two of them (Am7 and Bm7) are right next to each other. This opens up a great opportunity to exploit the geography of the guitar fretboard: any Am7 arpeggio licks you know can be moved up a whole step and repeated for Bm7. We don't want to get ahead of ourselves, but begin to think about these musical possibilities.

Learning the superimposed diatonic arpeggios

Now we're going to take an organized approach to learning the sound of each diatonic arpeggio in the parent key of G Major by playing it up and down over a funky Am7 groove. Notice which arpeggios prick up your ears, either positively or negatively. As soon as you hear a sound you like, explore it and begin to make some melodies with it.

Let's begin with GMaj7 over Am.

The hack to access this sound quickly is to think Am7 with its root on the fifth string, 12th fret, and move down a whole step to launch the GMaj7 arpeggio from the 10th fret.

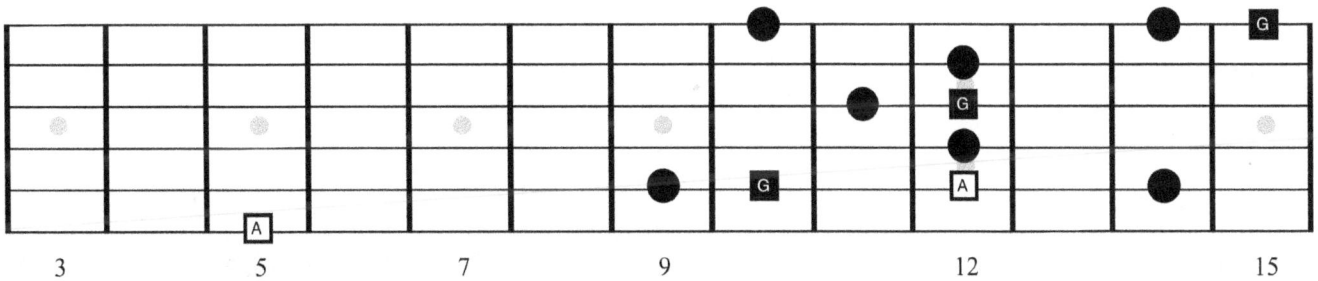

Example 1h

There's no hack for playing Am7 over Am7! Just play the minor arpeggio from the root. It still sounds good, but it's safe and it might be a little predictable.

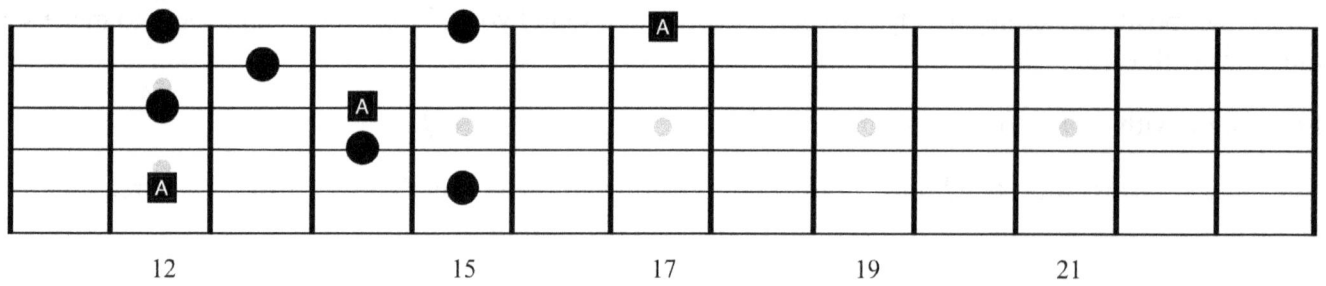

Example 1i

Superimposing Bm7 over Am7 creates some interesting extended harmony, and it's useful to know there are two minor arpeggios we can access that are a whole step apart. You'll often hear me move sequences up and down between the two. The quick hack is just to move up a whole step from the root.

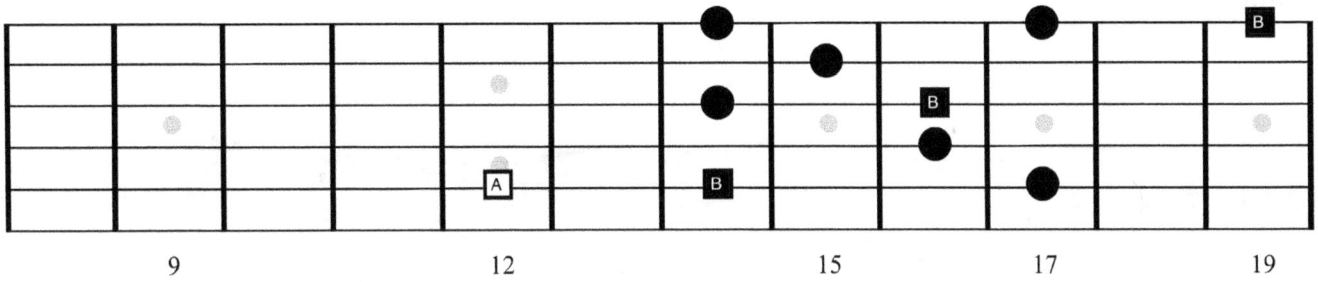

Example 1j

CMaj7 over Am7 is a really important sound and often one of my first choices. To make this work in any key, the hack is to picture the minor pentatonic scale, then go down two frets from the first note on the fifth string to play a Maj7 arpeggio.

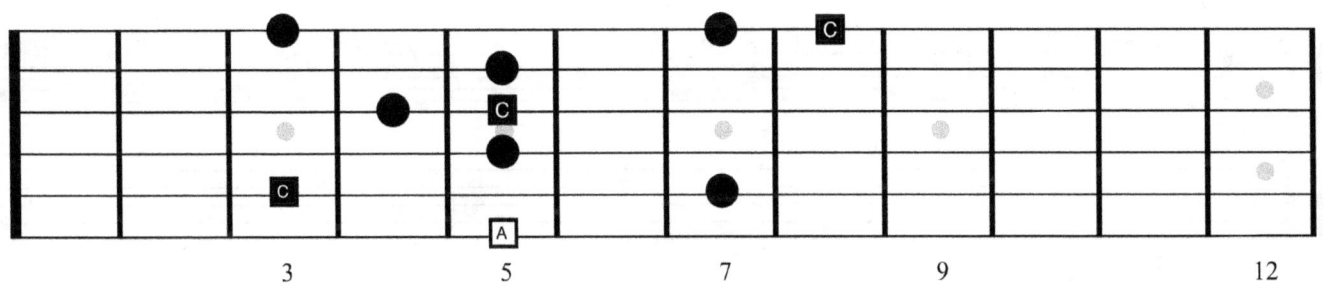

Example 1k

Cmaj7/A

(guitar notation and tablature)

Next, try D7 over Am7 and see what you think of the sound. The quick access hack is to move across a string from the sixth string root of Am.

(fretboard diagram)

```
3        5        7        9        12
```

Example 1l

D7/A

(guitar notation and tablature)

Em7 over Am7 is one of my first choices of soloing color. Remember the hack is to picture the A Minor Pentatonic scale box and play the Em7 arpeggio two frets higher on the fifth string.

Example 1m

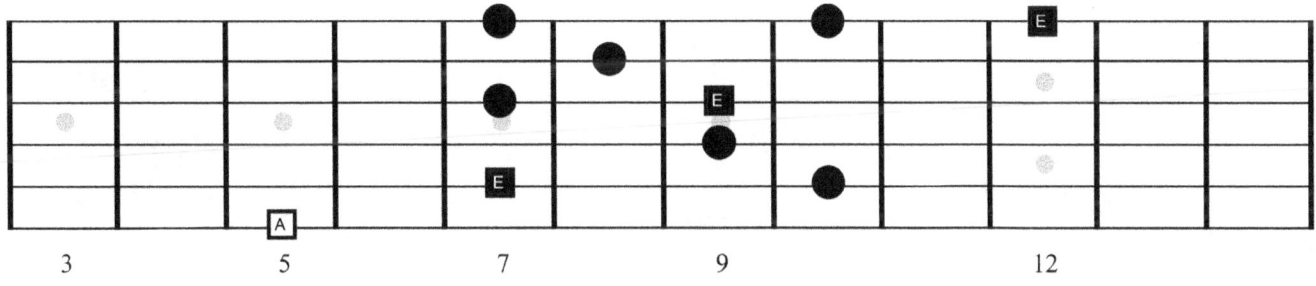

```
Em7/A
          7—10  12—10—7                7-10-12-10-7
        8             8              8            8
      9     9—7                    7-9    9—7
   7—10         10   7—10            9        9
                        10 7—10              10
```

```
      7-10-12-10-7                        7-10-12-10-7
    8           8                       8           8
  7-9   9—7                  7-9-7    7-9   9—7
9     9     10  7—10      9        9      9      10  7
   7-10           10  7—10  7-10
```

19

Finally, F#m7b5 is a very cool sound to try over the Am7 chord. The hack is to go down three frets from the Am7 root on the fifth string. The A note is on the 12th fret, so play the m7b5 arpeggio shape from the 9th fret.

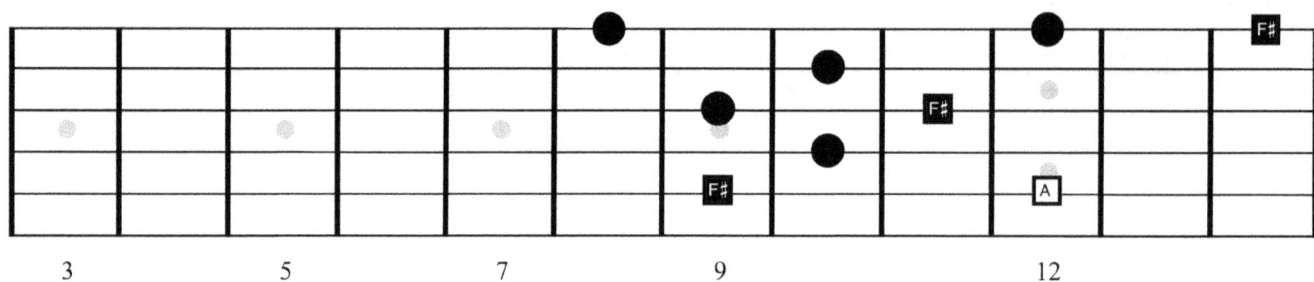

Example 1n

Let's summarize what we've learned so far.

1. All the arpeggios and chords in a parent key are strongly related because they share the same "pool" of seven notes. This means that an arpeggio built on *any note* of the G Major scale can be used to outline rich colors over *any chord* in the key of G Major.

2. Playing a different arpeggio over a chord is called *superimposing* because you're layering one sound up over another

3. Some arpeggio superimpositions sound better or more interesting than others, so you need to use your ears.

4. These arpeggios act as a musical scaffolding or framework. They are colorful *target* notes that you can use to build melodies

5. As each arpeggio is fingered in a consistent way, they interlock perfectly with the melodic scales and ideas I'll introduce later.

I remember the moment I discovered arpeggio superimposition. I was listening to guys like Frank Gambale and Brett Garsed, thinking to myself, "My technique is as good as theirs, so why don't I sound as musical?"

The realization came when I began *transcribing* their music. I could immediately see them using very clear arpeggio shapes in their playing, but they weren't the ones I was expecting! Instead of playing Am7 arpeggios over Am7 grooves, they were using arpeggios like GMaj7, CMaj7, Em7 and F#m7b5, which created an advanced, modern sound.

When I realized that these arpeggios came from the same parent key of G Major, my playing changed so quickly it was like seeing The Matrix! I began trying out these ideas and instantly discovered a whole new level of musicality in my playing. Instead of repeating the predictable sounds and melodic ideas I'd used before, I had found a new palette of rich musical colors to paint with. It totally changed the way I saw the fretboard and understood music.

The great thing was that I'd already figured out how to play all the arpeggios in my own consistent way, so it was just a case of physically moving my existing arpeggio language to a new place on the fretboard.

In the rest of this book, we're going to go deeper into this idea and I'll show you how I build lines around arpeggios using my own scale fingerings, chromatic ideas, and much more.

When you've memorized the arpeggio shapes on the previous pages, move on to the next section where we'll start to make some real music with them.

Musical Application of Superimposed Arpeggios

In the previous section you auditioned the sounds of superimposed arpeggios and learned to play them in a simple way over an Am7 vamp. Now we need to develop these arpeggio choices in a musical way, smoothly integrating them into our playing.

In order to introduce each arpeggio so it sounds like a natural part of our soloing vocabulary, we'll surround it with strong A Minor Pentatonic or Blues scale licks and phrases. There is a lot of great language to be drawn from just those two scales, and we'll use it to *frame* our superimposed arpeggios so help guide our audience into the more advanced sounds.

So we're all on the same page, I'll start by showing you some A Minor Pentatonic ideas that I might typically play. They're based around the 5th fret position on the neck and played using the classic pentatonic box shape you might consider "home territory". Use this as an opportunity to hear how they sound against the Am7 backing track and to learn a bit of my language. These licks will become a jumping off point from which you can begin to explore the superimposed arpeggios.

Example 1o:

Example 1p:

Example 1q:

So far, so good. We've got a few strong phrases we can use over the Am7 vamp, so now let's elevate it by exploring everything you've just learned in this chapter.

Just as we think of the minor pentatonic scale box as a "territory" on the guitar, superimposed arpeggios open up a range of new territories to explore, leading us to target different notes and colors in our melodies. These arpeggios don't just introduce new colors, they become four-note skeleton structures in their own right – a framework that we can flesh out with scale notes, chromatic ideas, melodic patterns and licks.

In other words, the arpeggio choice brings the *tonality*, and the modifications (scale notes, chromatic notes etc.) bring the *personality*.

The following examples begin with a strong pentatonic melody will give your ears a chance to get used to the tonality before the superimposed arpeggio idea adds the new colors. We'll leave the D7 arpeggio to one side in these examples, as it's the least useful of our available options.

The first line begins with some A Minor Pentatonic phrases, then introduces a CMaj7 arpeggio lick over the Am7 vamp. You'll immediately hear the richer note choices over the backing. This is followed by more pentatonic vocabulary before we return to the Cmaj7 arpeggio.

The CMaj7 arpeggio contains the notes C, E, G and B. Three of these notes (C, E and G) belong to the Am7 chord. The added B note introduces the beautiful sounding 9th interval above the A root note.

Example 1r:

Let's pick a different arpeggio and see how it sounds over Am7. Here's F#m7b5 which contains the notes F#, A, C and E. Three notes are in the Am7 chord (A, C and E) but the F# is an extended note and introduces the 6th interval of the scale. Again, I begin with a minor pentatonic idea before moving into F#m7b5 territory. I also break up the arpeggio a little rhythmically which helps it to blend more naturally into the overall picture.

Example 1s:

Next, here's another short solo that begins in A Minor Pentatonic line, then moves into an idea based around the Em7 arpeggio (E, G, B, D). Em7 has two notes that aren't contained in the Am7 harmony: the B note we've already seen that creates a 9th interval, and a D note which is the 11th of Am7.

Example 1t

How about playing GMaj7 (G, B, D, F#) over Am7?

This time there is just one note in common with the Am7 chord (G), and we add the B, D and F# color notes we've used all together: the 9th, 11th and 13th. I love this sound – I think you'll agree that it's the most sophisticated sounding superimposition so far.

Example 1u:

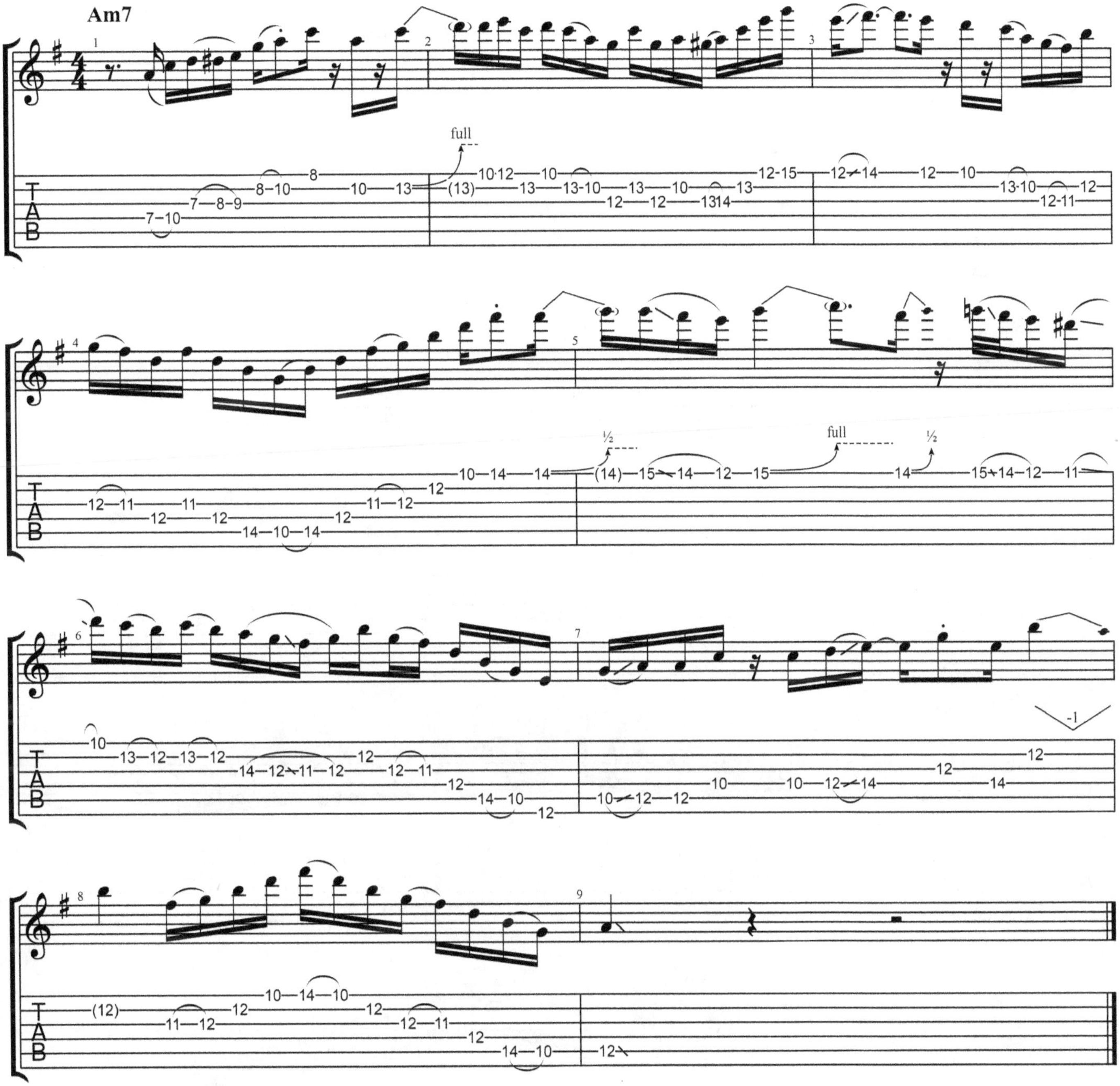

Another cool sound is to play the Bm7 arpeggio over Am7. The notes in Bm7 are B, D, F and A which give us, in order, the 9th, 11th, 13th and root. This superimposition is great for moving sequential melodic ideas up and down a whole step between Bm7.

Here's an example that introduces the Bm7 arpeggio over the Am7 vamp.

Example 1v:

Now it's over to you. Pick one arpeggio at a time and use it to solo over the Am7 backing track. Keep playing for as long as you can, because I want you to *hear* for yourself how these arpeggios sound in context.

You might find that some of these are easier on the ear than others to begin with, but even if an arpeggio choice doesn't immediately strike you, stick with it for a while, because new sounds can take a while to settle. We will use these arpeggio shapes in lots of other ways later, so it's important to be familiar with them all, even if they don't grab you to begin with. I suggest you spend some time with CMaj7, then Em7, then F#m7b5, then GMaj7 before tackling Bm7 and D7.

The process to get you started is to play an A Minor Pentatonic idea, then follow it with a superimposed arpeggio idea, then return to a minor pentatonic idea if you want to. You can spend as long as you like exploring each arpeggio.

Another important hack to know is that once you've set up a superimposed sound, it's quite easy to connect up all the arpeggios and play them up and down the neck, so that you take your listener on a journey using the full range of the guitar.

In this chapter we've explored how each of the arpeggios in the parent key can be used to create a rich, expanded tonality against an Am7 groove. We then turned each one into a melodic idea by adding some scale notes and preceding each arpeggio with a minor pentatonic lick. However, I've not yet taught you much about how I combine scale ideas with arpeggio structures, so in the next section we'll discuss how I play my scale shapes, before we move on to discover how I approach building meaningful licks.

Chapter Two: Greg Howe Scale Shapes

Once you've got the arpeggio shapes under your fingers and you're beginning to hear the unique sounds they create when superimposed over the Am7 groove, it's time to start exploring the further melodic possibilities that are available by adding scale notes around them.

When it comes to scale patterns, it may surprise you to learn that I don't play the typical three-note-per-string patterns that are common in my genre of music.

Instead, I arrange my scales so that their fingerings lock in seamlessly with the arpeggio shapes we've just covered, and so that they take advantage of the natural tuning of the third (G) string.

One thing I never liked is how the common three-note-per-string scale shapes always force you diagonally upwards on the neck as soon as you hit the G string. I didn't like this because *I* wanted to be the one who controlled where I was playing on the guitar. Also, in many scale books, you'll often see scales that combine two-note- and three-note-per-string patterns, where the string with two notes changes every time. This didn't sit right with me as the uneven distribution of the notes across the strings ended up controlling how I phrased my melodies

For example, here's a common way that guitar students are taught to play the D Mixolydian shape of the G Major scale. Notice how arranging the scale this way forces your hand up the neck when you get to the G string.

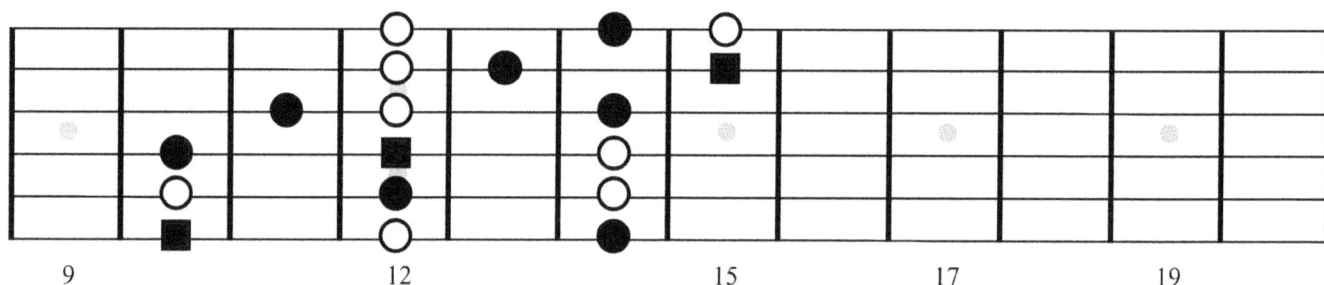

Compare that scale arrangement with how I organize the notes on the neck when I play in the same position. This small adjustment means that, not only can I stay in the same position without being forced up the neck, but the scale shape locks in perfectly with my arpeggio fingering (indicated by the black dots on the diagram).

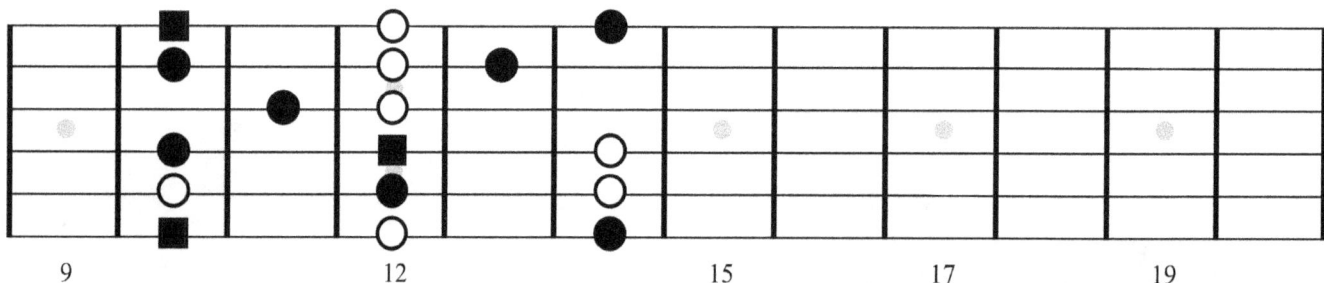

You can see that the scale shape locks in perfectly with my arpeggio, because both have two notes on the G string. What's more, the third string starts to function as a kind of "escalator" that allows me to shift positions on the neck easily and fluently. We'll explore this idea more in due course.

I know you've probably already spent a lot of time learning the seven shapes of the major scale modes, so you might be a little resistant to reorganizing your thinking. But I'll ask you to trust me here and see how this works out for you.

There are some small adjustments to be made to what you already know, but these patterns are incredibly powerful and will help you become a player who can switch between scale ideas and arpeggios seamlessly.

The following diagrams show you the seven patterns of the modes of the major scale that I use, played from the fifth string, but I've also highlighted the corresponding 5th string arpeggio shapes in black to show you how they perfectly lock together.

I'm teaching you these shapes from the fifth string to show you how the scales lock into the arpeggios, but I don't want you to neglect the 6th string, so when I descend the scale shape, I'll extend it back onto the 6th string.

In the notation below I play up and down each shape from the fifth string, then play the related arpeggio so you can see how they fit together. This is a great way to practice them.

Example 2a:

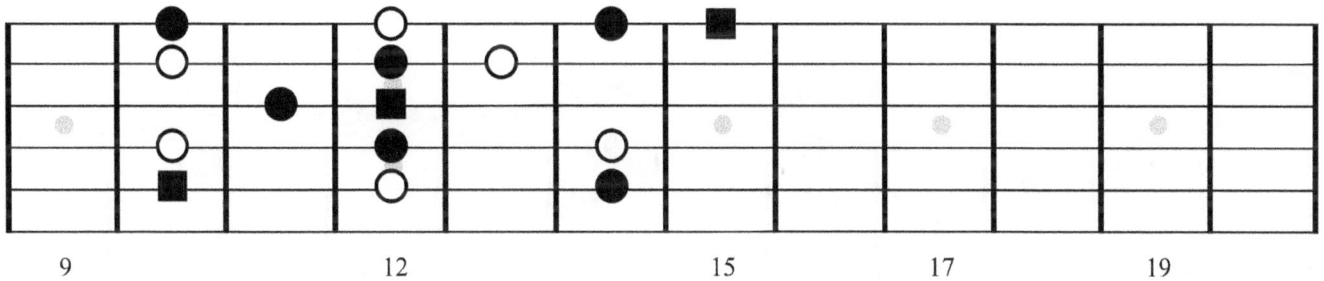

Example 2b:

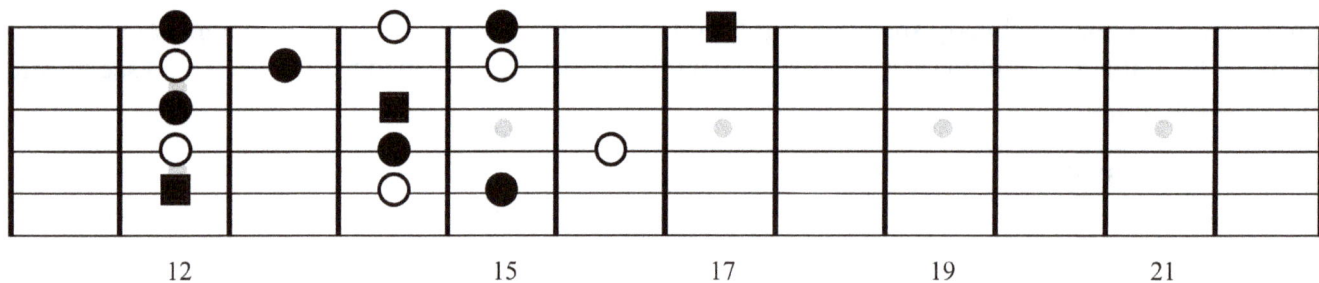

Example 2c:

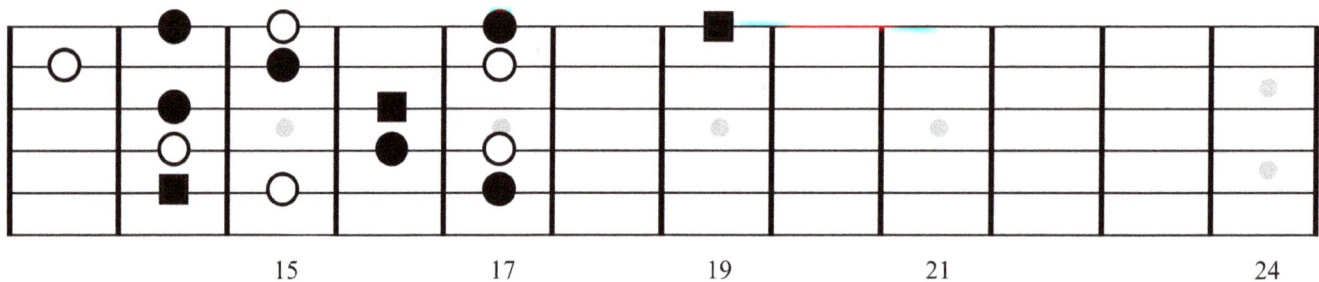

Example 2d:

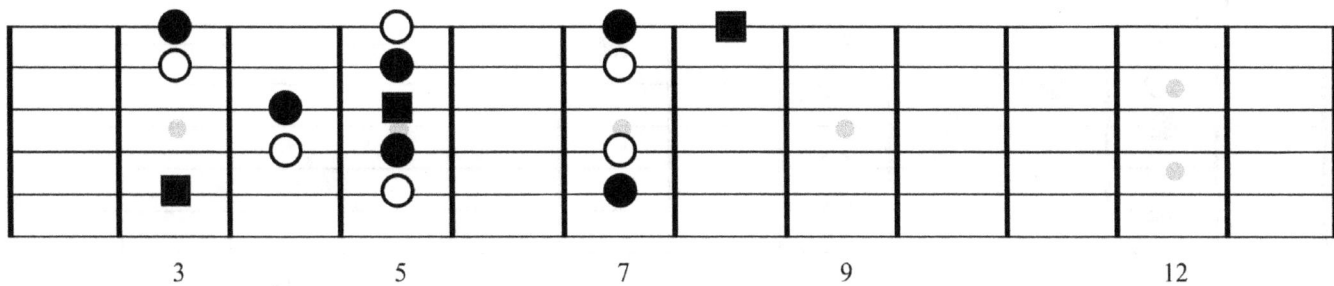

Example 2e:

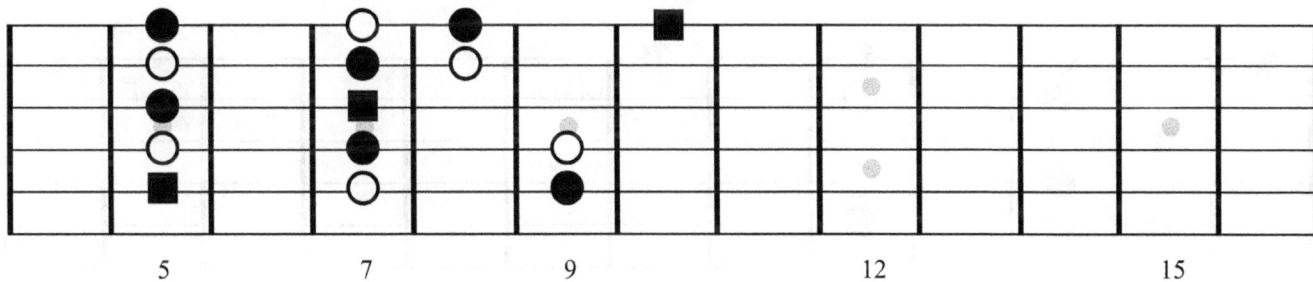

Example 2f:

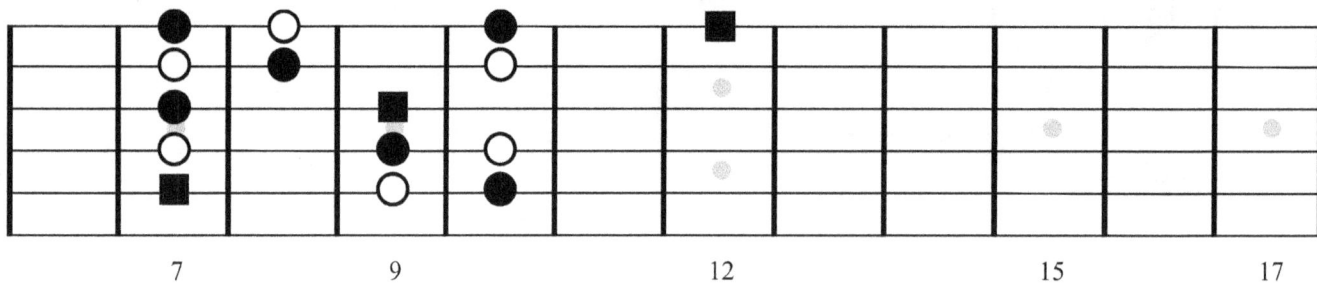

Example 2g:

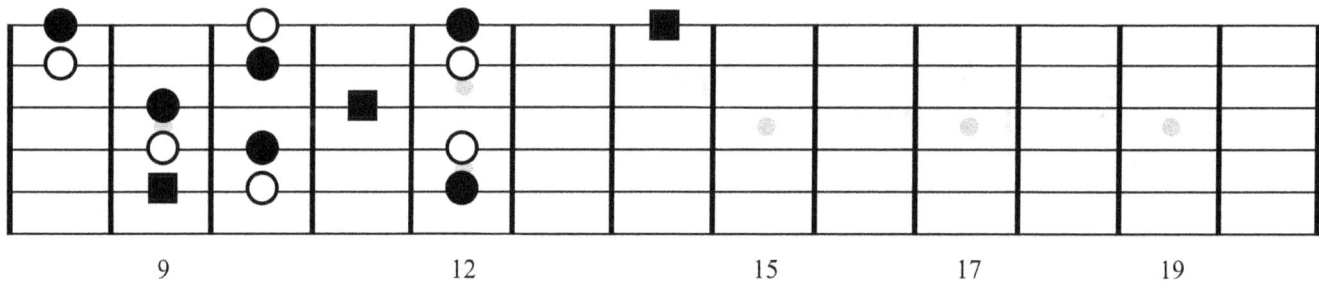

If you've never tried this way of playing scales/arpeggios before, the small adjustment needed to transition from the third to second string may take a little time to get used to, but I'm confident you'll pick it up quickly. In no time at all it will make a massive difference to your playing. Spend some time learning these shapes and switching between them and the arpeggios.

Try playing up the scale and descending the scale and vice versa. Also, look for points at which you can move between the scale and arpeggio easily in the middle of the shape. You can practice this logically by playing up the scale a different number of strings, then switching into the arpeggio.

To get you started, here are eight examples that begin with a scale melody then transition smoothly into the arpeggio before moving back to the scale.

There are two transitional ideas for each of the four arpeggio shapes and they are all played over our workhorse Am7 groove.

These first two ideas move in and out of the GMaj7 arpeggio.

Example 2h:

Example 2i:

The next two examples move in and out of the Em7 arpeggio.

Example 2j:

Example 2k

Now try moving in and out of the D7 arpeggio.

Example 2l:

Example 2m

And here is the F#m7b5 arpeggio.

Example 2n:

Example 2o:

Let's have a quick summary of where we are. You now know:

*   How to play all the arpeggio shapes

*   What it sounds like when you superimpose them

*   My economical Major scale modal shapes

*   How to move between the arpeggio shapes and the major scale shapes.

Now we can quickly get much deeper into the cool stuff – all the licks, patterns and language I build around the arpeggio shapes to make music.

Chapter Three: Designing Ascending Lines

We now know that we can play any arpeggio structure from the G Major parent scale to tonally color our melodies and solos against an the Am7 groove. We have also begun to transition smoothly between the four main arpeggio types and the G Major parent scales shapes that are built around them.

The great news is that you've done most of the groundwork and can now get onto the important (and fun!) business of building musical lines you can use in your songwriting and solos.

The method we'll be using is to *design* lines around the skeleton framework of the arpeggio shapes. This way we retain the tonality and color they offer against the backing while decorating them with scale ideas.

A good place to start is to learn to *disguise* the arpeggio by adding a short scale sequence or melody on different strings as you ascend the shape. To understand how this works, let's break down an idea based around the CMaj7 shape.

All I'm going to do is add a three-note scale idea before ascending through the arpeggio to the third string. Here's how it sounds.

Example 3a:

Now I'll add that pattern around the arpeggio notes on the third string, then continue up the arpeggio to the high E string where I repeat the sequence.

Example 3b:

While the two patterns on the fifth and third string are very similar, the slight difference makes for a more interesting lick. Now let's hear both sections combined.

Example 3c:

Let's review what's just happened here. We've taken the rich colors of the CMaj7 tonality over Am7 and *targeted* the arpeggio notes with the scale note pattern built around it. This is a huge key to how I construct my lines. I don't necessarily think *licks*, I think of short scalic *vocabulary* built around arpeggio colors.

The next mind-blowing concept to consider is that because our scales and arpeggios have a consistent fingering, you can play this exact pattern around *any* of the four arpeggio shapes, simply by adjusting the scale notes to fit the scale shape in the new position. Let me show you what I mean.

Here's that same pattern built around the Em7 arpeggio at the 7th fret.

Example 3d:

Now here's the pattern played around the F#m7b5 shape at the 9th fret.

Example 3e:

And here's the pattern around the D7 arpeggio shape at the 5th fret.

Example 3f:

We've just applied the same vocabulary to all four arpeggio types, and we've built lines around four very different superimposed colors over Am7 – all with the same basic melodic idea.

This is a very strong way to introduce this language into your playing and it gives you seven different-colored inflections on what is basically the same fingering and picking pattern.

The previous four examples covered arpeggios built on four of the seven notes of the parent key. We can, of course, use the same patterns on the other three notes, though we might need to make small adjustments to the melodic patterns to incorporate the slight differences in the scale shapes.

For example, if we play the Bm7 arpeggio, we have to make the following adjustment for the scale shape on the fifth and third strings.

Example 3g:

For this pattern, the Am7 and GMaj7 arpeggios would remain the same.

Example 3h:

```
T|---------------------------12-----|------------------------------10-|
A|--------------------13------------|---------------------------12----|
D|----------12-16-14-12-14----------|--------11-14-12-11-12-----------|
G|------14--------------------------|-----12-------------------------|
B|--12-15-14-12-15------------------|--10-14-12-10-14----------------|
```

Now you've got the idea, let's play this pattern on every single note ascending from the 3rd fret on the fifth string. i.e. From CMaj7 all the way up to Bm7 on the 14th fret.

In practical terms, I would rarely link together all my arpeggio lines with the same pattern – that would defeat the purpose of being able to cherry pick specific arpeggios to highlight certain colors in a solo. However, this is a great exercise to improve your visualization of the arpeggios across the fretboard, and also a very useful warm-up drill.

Example 3i:

```
T|------------------3-----|------------------5-----|------------------7-----|
A|------------5-----------|------------7-----------|------------8-----------|
D|----4-7-5-4-5----------|----5-9-7-5-7----------|----7-11-9-7-9----------|
G|--5--------------------|--7--------------------|--9--------------------|
B|--3-7-5-3-7------------|--5-9-7-5-9------------|--7-10-9-7-10----------|
```

```
T|------------------8-----|------------------10----|------------------12----|
A|------------10---------|------------12---------|------------13---------|
D|----9-12-11-9-11-------|----11-14-12-11-12-----|----12-16-14-12-14-----|
G|--10------------------|--12------------------|--14------------------|
B|--9-12-10-9-12--------|--10-14-12-10-14------|--12-15-14-12-15------|
```

```
T|------------------14----|------------------15----|
A|------------15---------|------------17---------|
D|----14-17-16-14-16-----|----16-19-17-16-17-----|
G|--16------------------|--17------------------|
B|--14-17-15-14-17------|--15-19-17-15-19------|
```

Now that we've covered the basic concept, here are four of my favorite ascending diatonic scale ideas built around the arpeggio of CMaj7.

Your job here is to first apply them to the other arpeggio *types*. Begin with Em7, D7 and F#m7b5, then play them on each of the seven notes of the scale, remembering to make any small adjustments necessary to play the correct notes in the parent key of G Major.

If you hear anything slightly off, it's probably because you're not making the correct adjustment to the scale pattern.

Here's a full neck diagram of G Major to help you find the correct notes.

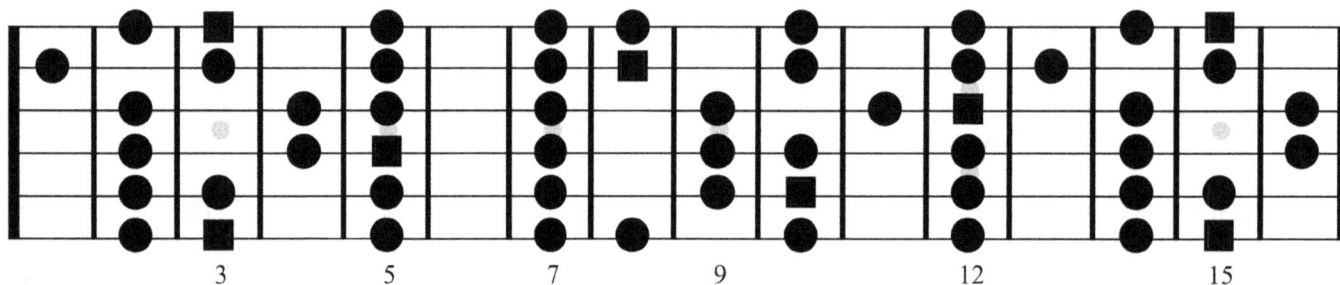

Example 3j:

Example 3k:

Example 3l:

Example 3m:

These four examples I've shown you are just the tip of the iceberg. They are just a few of the millions of potential melodic patterns you could add before, during, or after the arpeggio notes. It doesn't take much to disguise the arpeggio and you're only really limited by your own creativity.

When I examine my playing, I can see that the easiest modifications to make are on any string that does *not* contain one note. In other words, I tend to add these patterns on the fifth, third and first strings – although, of course, you can play whatever your ears tell you to.

I'd also like you to consider the fact that these melodic patterns are very long and don't often repeat in a perfect sequence, especially when we get to the third string.

While you and I know we're playing patterns based around scales and arpeggios, they are less predictable and much longer than the kinds of four-note sequences you might hear in a classic rock or neoclassical track. For this reason, they're very hard to for the average listener to spot and sound much more musically fluid.

So, not only are we introducing sophisticated colors into our playing by using selective arpeggios, we're also disguising them with long, articulate, slightly unpredictable, and much more melodic ideas. Cool huh?!

Now it's over to you.

Experiment with this and go write some of your own scale ideas around an arpeggio. Then translate them to the other shapes in the G Major parent key. Begin with melodic patterns that are short and similar on the fifth, third and first strings, but then try playing a different pattern on one of those strings, before playing slightly longer scale ideas.

Don't forget to jam out these ideas with the backing tracks, to help you play them in a musical way and to "audition" them around your preferred arpeggio substitutions.

To get you started, here's one idea that decorates the fourth string.

Example 3n:

The next stage is to learn to incorporate these ideas smoothly into our playing, so that we can control when they make an appearance in our solos. You'll remember from the first chapter that if we introduce these ideas "unprepared" they can sometimes sound a little forced or awkward; especially at first, when you're just getting a handle on things.

So, to learn these ideas smoothly, let's go back to our method of playing an A Minor Pentatonic lick before the arpeggio-based idea, then resolving it. This is a more natural and "safe" way to prepare the listeners' ears before taking them on a musical journey with your melody.

I'm going to use the first pattern we covered in Example 3c as a workhorse, but you should apply the following process to all the examples in this chapter before doing it with your own decorated arpeggio ideas.

Let's begin by playing an A Minor Pentatonic idea, then transitioning into the pattern around an Em7 arpeggio.

I have taken a more flexible musical approach to the following exercises, so you'll hear that I don't always play the arpeggio section of the lick exactly as written in Example 3c. Just use this as an opportunity to learn a little bit more of my musical vocabulary.

Example 3o:

Now here's a similar idea around the CMaj7 arpeggio.

Example 3p:

This time let's try the pattern around the F#m7b5 arpeggio.

Example 3q:

Now repeat this process for the other arpeggios in the parent key of G Major before trying it with the other melodic patterns we've covered and also combining it with your own original ideas.

Combined arpeggios

Now let's take things a bit further. We're going to create some melodic lines that combine *adjacent arpeggio pairs*.

In the following example, I begin with a minor pentatonic idea, transition into the F#m7b5 arpeggio, move up into the GMaj7 arpeggio, then resolve the idea to create a longer, more complex line.

Notice both *how* and *where* I change positions between the two shapes. Once you're comfortable with this idea, repeat the process with some of the melodic ideas from earlier in the chapter. Next, see if you can expand this concept into different adjacent arpeggio pairs to create your own longer lines.

Example 3r:

Here are a few more of my favorite ascending movements that transition between adjacent arpeggios. These are just ideas to get you started and help you understand how smoothly we can move between shapes.

As you get more comfortable with these sounds, you'll be able to omit a lot of the minor pentatonic phrases and deal with the superimpositions more naturally.

The first movement shifts between the Am7 and Bm7 arpeggios.

Example 3s:

This idea ascends from GMaj7 to Am7.

Example 3t:

This idea begins on CMaj7 and ascends quickly to Em7.

Example 3u:

Now begin making similar shifts using the different melodic scale patterns from earlier in the chapter before trying your own ideas. Remember that you don't sequence the same decoration identically on the fifth, third and first strings. In fact, adding a bit of variation or being somewhat loose with the pattern will often create more musical results.

For the final few examples in this chapter I want to mix things up a bit by showing you a few more ways to shift between arpeggio and scale ideas. To do this, I'm going to play more scalic ideas that ascend the lower strings before transitioning into arpeggio ideas on the higher strings. I don't want you to think that the lick structures we've covered so far are all I play!

This decorated pattern works its way from the fifth string to the third until it ascends a CMaj7 arpeggio (spanning the end of bar one into bar two) with one added passing note. Then, two higher notes target the B of the CMaj7 and we play an inversion of the arpeggio to start the descending run, which is followed by an Em7 inversion.

Example 3v:

In this example, we spend even longer working with an A Dorian scale sequence until we ascend a GMaj7 arpeggio on beat 2 of bar two, and descend an Am7 inversion just after beat 3.

Example 3w:

Here is another useful A Dorian sequence, this time launched from the b3 of the underlying Am7 chord. It climbs gradually until we ascend, then descend an F#m7b5 arpeggio halfway through bar two.

Notice that with each of these last three ideas, I've sought to conclude the line by landing on a strong chord tone of Am7 – in each case, the root note, though the 3rd would have been an equally good option. An important principle of extending or going outside of the harmony is to come back inside on a strong beat to ground the idea for your listeners.

Example 3x:

We'll end this chapter with a sixteen-bar study piece that links together all of these ideas. On the audio, I played this etude free time, to my own tempo, without backing, as my purpose here is not to teach you a solo. This is an extended exercise for you to work through, that shows how I set about playing arpeggio patterns all over the neck.

The exercise will help you to link together arpeggio lines in different zones of the fretboard, and also help you to build fluency in executing these shapes. I played the exercise at a reasonably quick pace on the audio, but you should work through it slowly, allowing your muscle memory to develop, before you think of speeding it up.

I'd also like you to do a bit of detective work yourself on this exercise!

When you spot an obvious arpeggio pattern, I want you to stop and work out which arpeggio is being played. To make this task less daunting, below is a table to refer to, containing the notes of each diatonic arpeggio in the key of G Major.

Bear in mind that at times I will play arpeggio inversions, so you're just looking for four notes in sequence that match one of the arpeggios below. For example, starting on beat 2 of bar three of the etude, you'll see that I play the notes B, G, E, D descending. This is an Em7 arpeggio inversion. Work through it and see what else you can discover!

GMaj7	G	B	D	F#
Am7	A	C	E	G
Bm7	B	D	F#	A
CMaj7	C	E	G	B
D7	D	F#	A	C
Em7	E	G	B	D
F#m7b5	F#	A	C	E

Example 3y:

In the next chapter I'll talk more about my approach to playing descending ideas using this system, but for now, your job is to see how many short scale ideas you can add to ascending arpeggio lines and start to use them in your own improvisation.

Chapter Four: Designing Descending Lines

In the previous chapter I showed you my approach to decorating and disguising arpeggio lines with short scale sequences. We also looked at some simple ideas you can use to create long patterns that don't repeat in a predictable way.

In the etude at the end of Chapter Three, you played a long sequence in which I ascended and descended arpeggios. In this chapter, we're going to look at my approach to building *descending* lines in more detail and examine a few differences that you can apply to create your own unique melodies.

You might expect that this chapter will simply contain many of the previous ideas played in reverse. While we will certainly cover a few lines like this to begin with, when I analyze my playing it's clear to me that I unconsciously take a different approach when playing descending lines with superimpositions, so we'll quickly move on to some typical lines that'd I'd actually play on a track.

Let's begin with a few short melodic scale patterns built around the CMaj7 arpeggio that mirror the approach we took earlier. We'll play a short melodic line to disguise the arpeggio on the first, third and fifth strings.

Launching from a G note on the first string (the b7 of the Am7 harmony), we play a nine-note descending scale sequence that flows into a CMaj7 arpeggio inversion played from its 7th, ending with the root note on the fifth string, 3rd fret.

Example 4a:

This pattern launches from the Am7 root note on the first string. When we get to the CMaj7 arpeggio (last four notes of measure one), we begin with the C root, but the remaining notes are played out of sequence. It's not so much an inversion as a four-note cell comprising the notes of CMaj7.

Example 4b:

It sounds nice to begin the scale sequence from a B note on the first string, which over Am7 implies an Am9 harmony. The descending sequence flows straight into a CMaj7 inversion played from its 7th.

Example 4c:

So far, so good. In your practice sessions, work on applying these patterns to the other diatonic arpeggio shapes beginning with Em7, F#m7b5 and D7. Try and create your own variations.

In the next three examples I use similar patterns around different arpeggios and precede each one with a pentatonic idea to form a cohesive melodic line that I might play in a solo. Again, learn these ideas then try them on different arpeggios and with your own variations.

The first line moves from a minor pentatonic idea into a descending melodic Em7 four-note cell phrase.

Example 4d:

This idea incorporates a descending CMaj7 phrase – the same four-note cell we used in Example 4c.

Example 4e:

This lick moves from A Minor Pentatonic into a descending GMaj7 phrase.

Example 4f:

The previous few lines were based around the same method as the ascending arpeggio ideas in Chapter Three: play a short scale idea on specific strings to embellish and disguise the superimposed arpeggio.

You should explore these concepts, as you'll get a lot of mileage out of them. However, when I analyze my own playing, I notice that my descending phrases often contain more scalic lines than arpeggios (although I do still move in and out of arpeggio ideas a great deal).

To show you what I mean, here are some more descending lines that I would typically play. I've written them around different arpeggio shapes, but the same principle of applying the patterns to every arpeggio shape still applies.

Once you've got your fingers around each one, apply it to a different arpeggio and adapt it to fit the G Major parent scale.

The first line descends around the CMaj7 arpeggio.

Example 4g:

This idea descends around the Em7 arpeggio.

Example 4h:

Here's something I like to play when descending around the F#m7b5 arpeggio.

Example 4i:

This descending scale line is built around The GMaj7 arpeggio.

Example 4j:

Finally, here are a couple of descending ideas that link together two adjacent arpeggios. This one connects GMaj7 and F#m7b5.

Example 4k:

This line links the arpeggios of CMaj7, Bm7 and ends back on Am7.

Example 4l:

As we've done previously, the next stage is to learn to transition into these kinds of lines from minor pentatonic vocabulary. I won't demonstrate this with every example, but here's a smooth way to get into a descending arpeggio lick from a minor pentatonic phrase. This short solo is built around Em7 over the Am7 backing.

Example 4m:

This chapter has been a little shorter, but that's because we've already nailed the main concepts and I'm sure you're starting to get a good idea of how you can develop your own descending lines by adding scalic ideas to the arpeggio on the first, third and fifth strings. Don't let that stop you from exploring melodic ideas on other strings, but these are a good place to start.

Remember, I suggest exploring two approaches:

1. Playing a short scale phrase on the arpeggio strings that contain just one note.

2. Playing more scalic ideas that eventually transition into an arpeggio movement.

As you become more confident, you'll probably be able to play fewer pentatonic phrases and be able to control the superimposed colors more.

In the next section we're going to look at how you can introduce chromatic notes (notes from outside the key) to create a dynamic, edgy sound.

Chapter Five: Chromatic Ideas and Other Shapes

We've looked at some solid ways to build strong ascending and descending lines using superimposed arpeggios combined with notes from the parent scale. Now, I want to show you how to play a little further out from the key center by introducing chromatic notes to add even more color and movement to our lines.

Often people assume there must be a ton of theory to understand when it comes to playing chromatic ideas, but really it's just a case of filling in the scale steps with a *passing note*, or playing one of a few common *chromatic approach patterns* that introduce outside notes in a way that is logical and melodic to the ears.

First, let's look at some lines that include a passing note.

In its simplest form, this just means that instead of playing, for example, the notes C to D in your melody, you fill in the gap with a chromatic C# note and play C, C#, D.

Anywhere there is a two-fret step in the scale, you can fill the gap in the middle.

If you filled in *all* the gaps, then essentially you'd be playing the Chromatic scale!

Here are two simple scale melodies that fill in some scale step gaps with chromatic notes. One ascends and the other descends. Notice that the chromatic notes tend to fall *off* the beat, which is great place to start learning to use these ideas. As your ears become more accustomed to the sound, you'll learn to place them on the beat too.

Here's the ascending line:

Example 5a:

And now the descending line:

Example 5b:

As you can see, there's no difficult theory here. To play chromatic notes I've just filled the gaps in the scale by playing a note in the middle. It's that simple.

The easiest way to understand *how* I use chromatic passing notes melodically is to learn some of my vocabulary to begin with, and absorb it into your playing. The following two lines use arpeggios and short scale phrases as before, but this time I add in some chromatic passing notes too.

The first line is ascending, based on the arpeggio of CMaj7.

Example 5c:

The next phrase is descending, based on the arpeggio of Em7.

Example 5d:

You can learn these two ideas as fingering patterns, then apply them to the other arpeggios in the parent key of G Major.

Here is a descending lick built around the GMaj7 arpeggio.

Example 5e:

This lick is built around the descending F#m7b5 arpeggio.

Example 5f:

The next useful way to add chromatic notes to scale phrases is to use *approach note* patterns. As the name suggests, this concept involves targeting chord/arpeggio tones by approaching them chromatically.

If this sounds very similar to what we just did, the distinction here is that we will often place an approach note a half step below an arpeggio note. This will create a new type of "outside-inside" pattern that weaves around the arpeggio tones. A slightly more dissonant sound can be produced by placing the approach notes a half step *above* the arpeggio tones.

Again, chromatic approach notes are normally played on a weak beat to begin with, but as you gain confidence you'll find you can place them anywhere you like in your phrases.

Now, here are nine melodic lines that demonstrate this concept. We'll kick off with a pattern that I really like to use.

A Dorian scale notes provide the framework for this line which begins on F# on the fourth string (for a minor 6 sound over the A minor harmony). You can see that on the third string, we're working around the same three-note skeleton, with notes on the 4th, 5th and 7th frets, but this time we decorate it with other notes. Notice in particular the chromatic C# note that connects D and C scale tones.

From beat 3 in bar one, we ascend a CMaj7 arpeggio. Often, in my playing, you'll see me ascend an arpeggio but place an additional scale tone before the last note of the arpeggio. Here, instead of playing straight up C, E, G, B, I played C, E, G, A, B. It feels natural to do this here, because we're filling the gap between the 3rd and 7th frets. What we've done here is to create a five-note CMaj13 arpeggio (the A note is the 13th), which is a sound that definitely appeals to me. The idea appears again in the conclusion of the line (the last five notes of bar two)

Example 5g:

Launching from the 5th of the Am7 chord, this scale sequence adds chromatic passing notes on the third and second strings, in bar one then bar two. Just before beat 4 of bar one, we ascend a D7 arpeggio.

Example 5h:

This line begins on the b7 (G) of the Am7 chord and goes straight into a chromatic descent, adding a non-scale tone (F) to add tension. Just before beat 3 we ascend an Em7 arpeggio. In the descending line that follows, notice the placement of four chromatic notes. These notes add some real downward momentum to the line and increase the tension that is finally resolved when we land on the A root note at the end of bar two.

Example 5i:

I really like the shape of this next line as a way of disguising an ascending then descending F#m7b5 arpeggio. The line ebbs and flows in a pleasing way, and just two chromatic notes are needed to fill out the 1/16th note pattern and add a little tension.

Example 5j:

In this line, as we ascend a GMaj7 arpeggio from beat 3 of bar one, I've used the same idea discussed in Example 5g, adding an E scale tone between the D and F# notes of the arpeggio to create a five-note GMaj13.

Example 5k:

This more agile line that has less note decoration at the beginning and moves across the strings more rapidly, shows another approach to disguising ascending and descending GMaj7 arpeggios.

Example 5l:

So far we've added a lot of chromatic approach notes above scale tones. This line uses chromatic approach notes from a half step below as well, specifically playing A# notes to target the B scale tone, a.k.a. the 9th of the underlying Am7 chord.

Example 5m:

This line weaves back and forth with an A Dorian scale sequence before playing a descending GMaj7 four-note cell, starting with the final note of bar one. Just before beat 2 of bar two, we ascend an F#m7b5 arpeggio. We ascend that arpeggio again in inversion form on beat 3& of bar two.

Example 5n:

In bar one of this final example, beginning on beat 2 I ascended an F#m7b5 arpeggio. The layout of the arpeggio on the high strings means that there is room to insert an extra scale tone (a D note between the C and E notes of the arpeggio). In the context of F#m7b5 this "filler" note represents a tense #5 interval, but since the line is played fast, the exciting tension is immediately resolved.

Example 5o:

These chromatic ideas are virtually limitless, because there are so many possible variations we could play. The lines I've shown you here are just the tip of the iceberg.

I want to round off this chapter by teaching you how to take the chromatic concepts we've learned and apply them to any area of the fretboard.

While the fifth string arpeggios we've covered are definitely an important feature of my approach to creating music on guitar (and were the starting point for my own exploration), I quickly found that the 2 1 2 1 2 arrangement of arpeggios (and the surrounding scale decorations) could be instantly applied to many other shapes on the guitar.

The following examples outline some of my favorite ideas based on this format. I begin each one with the pattern I use in its pure form. This is followed by a decorated version that will sometimes also contain chromatic notes.

I won't provide any further theory or explanation, because by now you know how to use these ideas and apply them in different areas. They're all played over the A minor backing track and are all taken from the G Major parent scale.

Example 5p:

Example 5q:

Example 5r:

Example 5s:

Example 5t:

Example 5u:

68

Example 5v:

Finally, here's a sixteen-bar study that brings together these ideas in an etude format.

Example 5w:

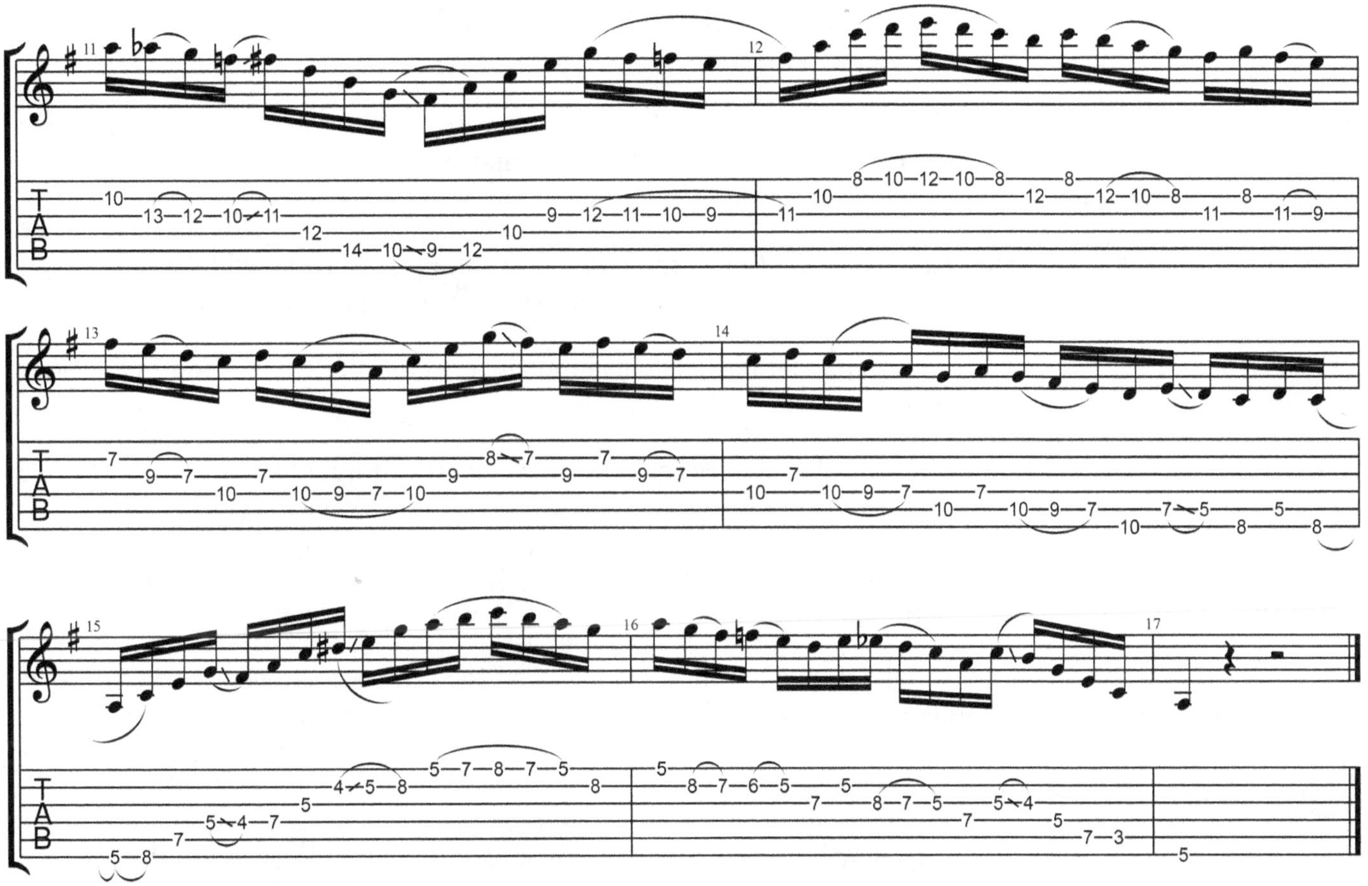

Chapter Six: Rhythm & Phrasing

The first five chapters of this book have covered a lot of ground in terms of my approach to arpeggio-based soloing on the guitar. You know which shapes I use, how to superimpose tonalities, and how to embellish or disguise these arpeggios with both scale and chromatic additions.

These five chapters are definitely a great grounding in modern guitar soloing, so you should definitely spend some time consolidating your learning, and work on those approaches for a while.

In this chapter, I want to discuss something that few students immediately consider when it comes to soloing – rhythm and phrasing.

Often, my students are so keen to get to the advanced melodic ideas that they forget the most important part of any solo is playing with *great time*.

In fact, you could go as far as to say that the *right* note played at the *wrong* time is still a "wrong note"! Because in music, phrasing is everything.

So, in this chapter we're going to take a break from arpeggios and look at some powerful ways you can add melodic leaps and a bit of unpredictability into your playing. The idea is to move away from *downbeat* phrasing, where all your melodies align predictably with the beat, and move towards *cross beat* phrasing where your playing has much more rhythmic interest.

The ideas and exercises in this chapter will show you a path towards much more interesting, rhythmically diverse music.

Let's begin with one of my favorite ways to disrupt the predictable phrasing of the A Minor Pentatonic scale and get away from the typical lines you'll hear with that scale.

The idea is really simple: play the A Minor Pentatonic scale along the third (G) string, and add the fifth interval above each note every time on the second (B) string. First, let's look at how these notes lay out on a map of the guitar neck.

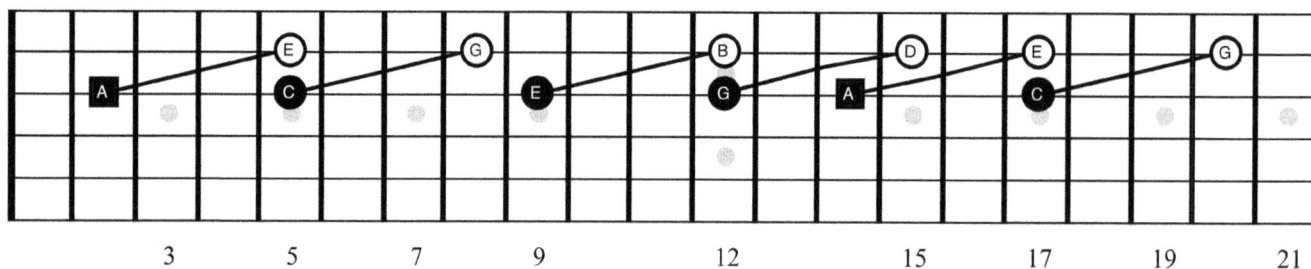

Begin by playing this exercise very smoothly and evenly. Start with the 2nd fret on the G string then play the 5th fret on the B string. Move up to the 5th fret on the G string then play the 7th fret on the B string. Repeat this pattern all the way up the neck as written below.

Example 6a:

Now let's make this a bit more interesting. Start with the note on the B string and descend down to the note on the G string. Slide up to the next pentatonic note on the G string, then play the next note on the B string. Now slide up on the B string and descend to the next pentatonic note on the G string.

This is definitely easier to see written down in notation than to explain in words, so play through the next example carefully.

Example 6b:

Here's a descending version of the previous idea.

Example 6c:

```
T|--22--------20--------17----------15--------12--------10-----------------8---------5--
A|-----19--17----17--14------14---12----12--9-----9--7-------7---5------5---2-------2---
B|------------------------------------------------------------------------------------
```

You can probably already hear that even by playing this idea in straight 1/8th or 1/6th notes, you're already messing with where the melodic phrasing would naturally fall. What's more, it sounds a lot different from the kind of bluesy pentatonic lines you'd normally play.

However, we can add another ingredient to the mix to create an even more angular approach. Let's add a high octave of the lower note and play it on the high E string.

This example shows you how to ascend and descend the A Minor Pentatonic scale between the octaves on the third and first strings

Example 6d:

```
T|----5-------8-------10------12------15------17-------20------17-------15------12------10----------8-------5--
A|--2--5-----5--7-----7---9----9--12----12-14----14-17--17-14----14-12----12-9----9--7----7---5----5--2------
B|-----------------------------------------------------------------------------------------------------------
```

```
T|----5-------8-------10-------12------15-------17------20------22-------20------17------15-------12------10------8-------5--
A|--2--2--5----5--7----7--9----9-12----12-14----14-17--17-19----19--17----17-14----14-12----12-9----9--7----7--5-----5--2---
B|--------------------------------------------------------------------------------------------------------------------------
```

Now that you have the root note, the fifth and the octave of A Minor Pentatonic all mapped out on the top three strings, let's look at some ways you can build unpredictable lines by moving between these notes while ascending and descending.

The first line begins on the fifth, moves down to the root, slides up to the next note of the pentatonic scale, jumps to the octave and then slides up again. This idea continues up the neck.

Example 6e:

Here are four different ideas that ascend or descend the neck with this idea of jumping between octaves, fifths and sliding. Once you get into this idea the possibilities are endless and you'll quickly come up with your own lines that contain big intervallic jumps with fun but unpredictable phrasing.

Despite these lines being purely pentatonic, we've easily moved way beyond blues licks and created a modern, fusion edge. I love these ideas because they make me sound like I'm thinking a lot more than I am!

Example 6f:

Example 6g:

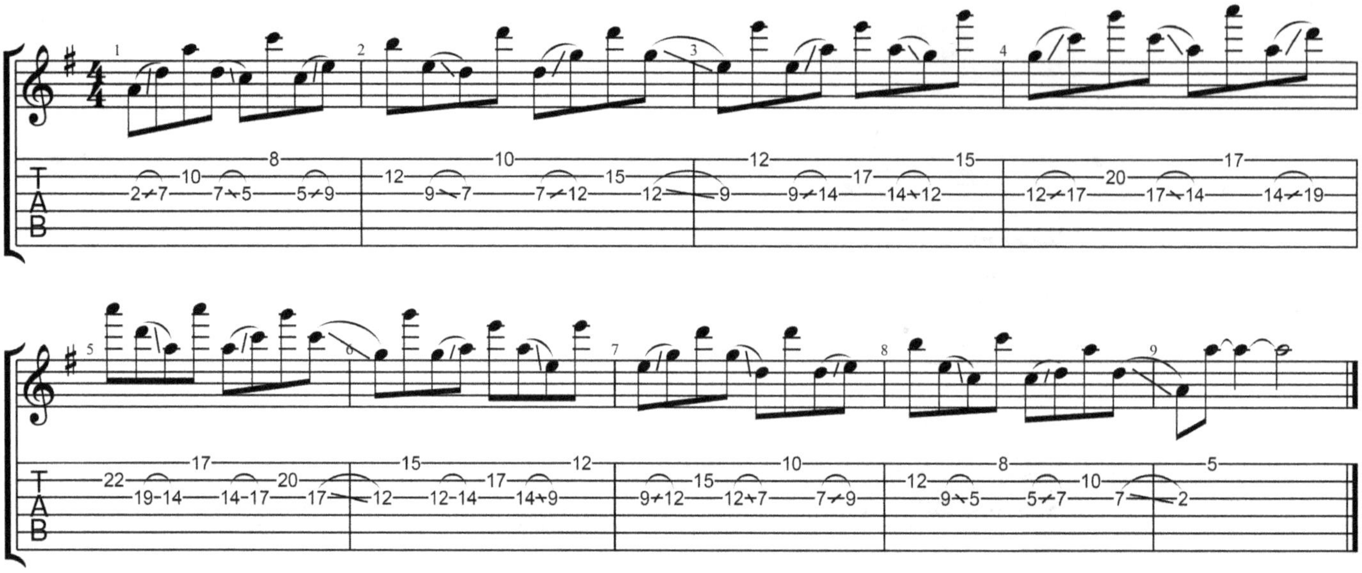

Example 6h:

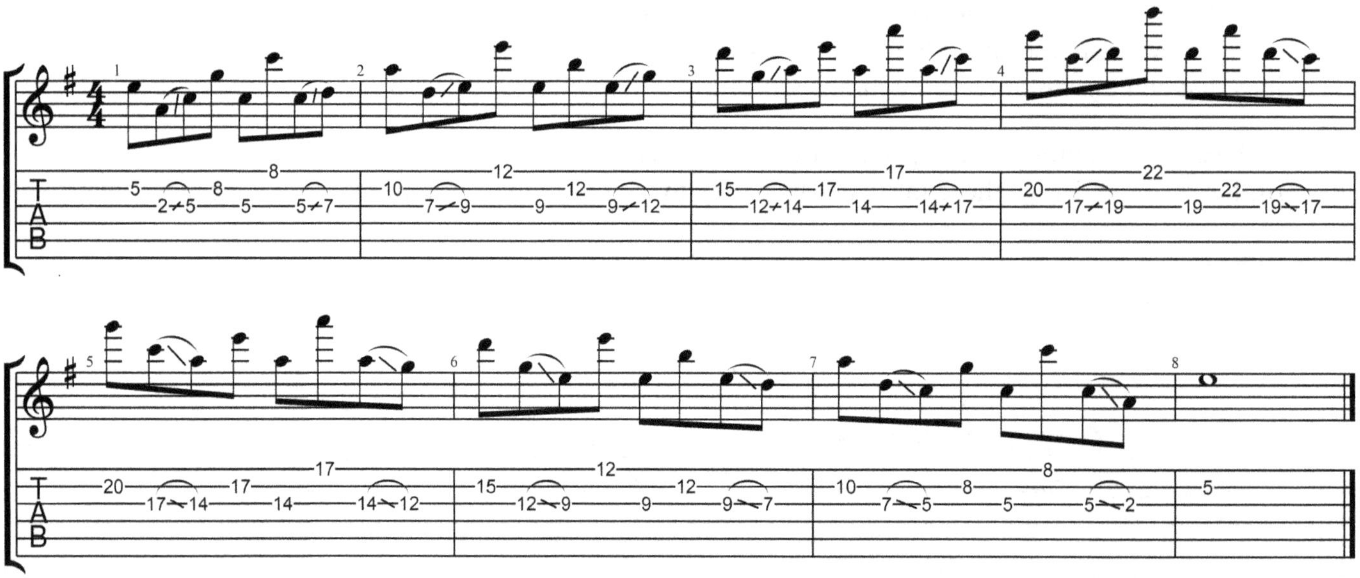

Example 6i:

It's important to point out that just like the arpeggio substitutions, these angular pentatonic lines need a bit of an introduction for your listener, so work on integrating them into your playing in a way that disguises them a little, just as we did with arpeggio patterns.

Chapter Seven: Cross-rhythmic Motifs

In this chapter I want us to continue to think about rhythm and phrasing. As guitarists, it's all too easy to get caught up in *what* notes we play and to forget about *how* we're playing them. When soloing, I like to use rhythmic ideas that play around with the time and shift across the beat. I find this a great way of introducing tension and melodic interest into a solo.

You probably already know that any phrase or lick you happen to play can be repeated and altered rhythmically to create a new idea. Blues players do this all the time, and they can get a lot of mileage out of every idea they play by moving the lick to different places in the bar, or altering the length of certain notes to alter the phrasing.

The way I approach creating rhythmic tension is a little different, and I want to pass onto you an advanced idea that has helped a great many students of mine break new territory on guitar – both rhythmically and harmonically.

In essence, it's the idea of creating a rhythmic motif that shifts across the beat. To do this, we start with a simple motif that, when played in a loop, creates a cross-rhythmic effect. It's an attention grabbing idea that can make your playing stand out from the ordinary.

In the examples that follow, I'll show you some cellular motifs that I like to use. You can practice these and add them to your vocabulary, but I also encourage you to work on inventing your own. In the examples that follow, I'll also include a couple of demonstrations that show how to integrate these ideas into a short solo.

Example 7a uses the following seven-note motif that includes some string-skipped intervals. The notes come from a superimposed Em7 arpeggio, and you can visualize this being based around an Em7 chord voicing in 7th position.

Since we're playing this line in 1/8th notes, every time we loop around the motif it's "pulled forward" by an 1/8th note and appears at a different place in the bar. Here's the motif played slowly.

Example 7a:

Now here's the motif looping around over our Am7 groove. Here it is played as 1/16th notes. You can hear that it has an almost hypnotic effect as we hear the repeated notes of the motif gradually shifting across the beat.

Example 7b:

Example 7c shows how we can take a motif like this and extend the idea by altering certain notes. We begin by playing the same motif as Example 7a. When it's repeated, the top note changes from a D to a C. The third time the motif is played, that top C changes to an A, and it's also played on the second string, so that we don't have to move our hand out of position.

Example 7c:

We can take these three iterations of the original motif and mix them up in any order we like to create a new, rhythmically exciting shifting idea.

Example 7d:

Example 7e shows how I might incorporate this motif-driven idea into a passage of a solo.

Example 7e:

You can get the most out of an idea like this by immediately applying it to another diatonic arpeggio from the parent key. Here we apply the pattern to an F#m7b5 arpeggio. Practice it slowly and get used to the sound of this new sequence. When you're comfortable, play it at tempo over our workhorse Am7 groove.

Example 7f:

We've tended to shy away from playing A minor arpeggios over Am7, but with the wider string-skipped intervals, it also sounds pretty good here!

Example 7g:

Now let's transfer this idea to superimpose a Bm7 arpeggio motif sequence over the Am7 groove. As before, learn it, get it up to speed, then try it out over the backing track.

Example 7h:

In this example, we return to the Em7 arpeggio, but played in a different zone of the neck and beginning on a different note. For practice, take the ideas we've used so far and see where else you can play them on the neck.

Example 7i:

```
Bar 1-3
T--------3-----------7------|------3---------5-----|------3---------7---------3-
A----4--7-------7--5----4---|---4--7-------5----4--|---7----4-------4--7--------
B---------------------------|---------------------|----------------------------
```

```
Bar 4-6
T--------7-------3------|---5-----5-------3-----|------7---------3-
A----7--5----4------4--7|-4-----4--7------5----4|----4------4--7----
B---7-------------------|---------7------------|------------------
```

Now let's look at a new idea. In this sequence, all the notes belong to an Em7add11 arpeggio (E, G, B, D, A) i.e. an Em7 arpeggio with an A note (11th) added in the upper octave.

Here we're using our motif template again, but disguising it by sandwiching it between some other scalic phrases. In fact, it's so well hidden it might be difficult to pick out on first listen! However, play from beat 3& in bar two (the motif begins with the final three notes of bar two) and you'll hear two iterations of the motif back to back.

Example 7j:

```
T------------------------------7-----------10----7---|----8----10------------------
A---------------7-------8--10------7---7--9---8------7-|--7----7----7----------------
B---7-10---7-10---10--7-9--7----7-9------9------7-9--9-|---------------9----10-----7-
```

Let's hear how this idea sounds, converted to 1/16th notes and played up to tempo.

Example 7k:

Next, we'll take this new pattern and apply it to the F#m7b5 arpeggio. First, practice the pattern in its new position. Then, gradually bring it up to tempo and practice it over the backing track.

Example 7l:

Now let's apply the pattern to an Am7 arpeggio.

Example 7m:

Here's the pattern using the CMaj7 arpeggio.

Example 7n:

Here's an example solo passage that has the Em7 arpeggio pattern embedded within it.

Example 7o:

This example has the CMaj7 pattern worked into a short solo passage.

Example 7p:

To end this chapter, Example 7q is a 32-bar study etude for you to work through in your practice sessions. It moves through the different rhythmic motifs we've worked on, but is arranged as one long, seamless exercise.

This will be challenging to learn and play up to tempo, but it will help you to refine both your rhythmic groove and picking technique.

First, listen to audio file Example 7q-1. This is the entire solo played slowly and unaccompanied. Use this to walk through the solo and learn it in manageable chunks at a comfortable pace.

When you've learned the whole thing, try playing along with me using audio file Example 7q-2, which is the solo up-to-tempo, played over the backing track.

If this seems like a big ask, don't be discouraged. It's fine to extract a few bars at a time from the solo and use them to jam over the backing track. My overall aim is to help you absorb these ideas into your vocabulary, then make them your own. Whatever works best for you is the best approach! Either way, make sure to have fun with it.

Example 7q:

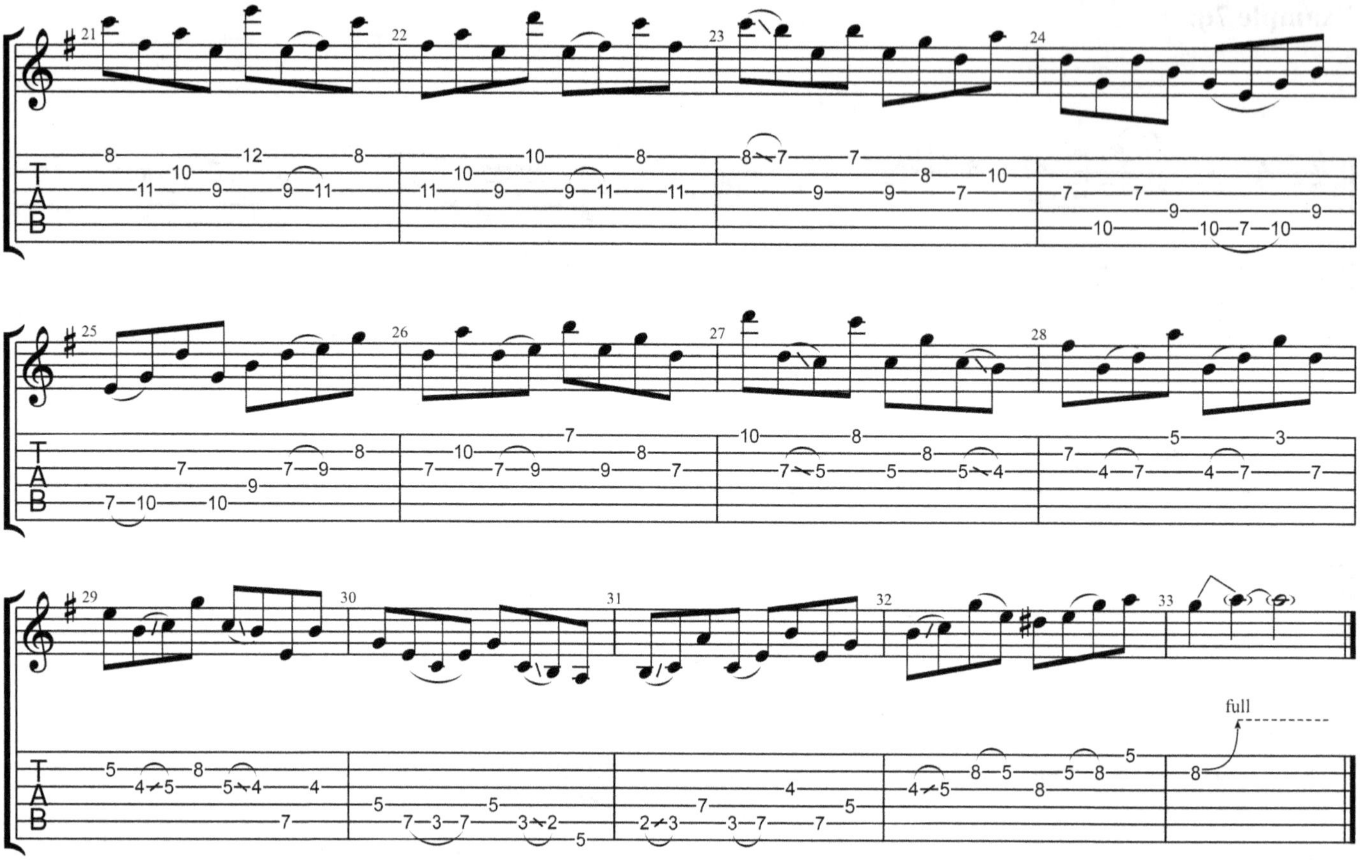
full

Chapter Eight: Performance Breakdown

To bring our journey to a close, I wanted to conclude with a performance that contains all of the ideas we've covered in this book, brought together in a spontaneously improvised solo over an Am7 vamp. This isn't a pre-planned or contrived "performance exercise" – it's exactly the kind of thing I would play from the heart if I was in your studio, you hit record, and you told me to just blow over the groove!

I've pulled out a few examples from the solo to highlight specific ideas. In these examples it's easier to see the thought process that went through my head – given all you now know about how I approach creating my melodic ideas.

The solo starts simply, but the opening phrase sets the tone for what's to come. Rather than beginning with a minor pentatonic lick, I opened with an ascending F#m7b5 arpeggio to create a more sophisticated Am13 sound, then was able to move naturally into some pentatonic vocabulary via a slide into an A note on the second string.

Example 8a

The next idea I'd like to draw to your attention occurs in bars 3-4 of the solo. This is a good example of the kind of chromatic lines I try to build into my solos. In the first measure, we have a cascading descending line, then in measure two I jump back onto the second string to play a pedal tone idea, bouncing off notes on the third string.

In measure one, the opening phrase (nine notes) is played with hammer-ons and pull-offs, and uses the notes of the A Blues scale. The next short phrase is an F#m7b5 arpeggio idea, where I target the F# note from a half step above, then I return to the A Blues scale for the remaining notes in this bar.

In measure two, I'm targeting that F# note again at the beginning of the bar to create a minor 6 or minor 13 color. The opening three-note phrase is repeated a half step down with chromatic notes, then shifts down again to land on an E note on the second string – the 5th of the Am7 chord.

Example 8b

In bars 6-8 of the solo, I play an ascending CMaj7 arpeggio into some wide bends, before playing a descending sequence. I'm using the A Blues scale again for this descending run.

Example 8c

Bar twenty-five of the solo begins with a scale sequence that moves into two disguised arpeggios. The first six notes of this lick come from the A Dorian scale. The next four notes ascend an Em7 arpeggio, and the four notes following on from that ascend a CMaj7 arpeggio, and a final Dorian scale note completes the run. I think this is as clear an example as you'll get of how to fuse together a scale fragment with two superimposed arpeggios to create a line that stands out over the Am7 groove. The second and third measures complete the idea with expressive bends.

Example 8d

One final example. Bars 31-33 contain one of the most difficult lines to play in the entire solo. There are two ideas on show here: first, an ascending GMaj7 arpeggio to begin the line, which as you'll recall highlight the 9th, 11th and 13th of the underlying Am7 chord – a beautiful sound. This connects with an Am triad, then the remaining notes in the first measure come from an F#m7b5 arpeggio disguised by chromatic notes.

In measure two, the second idea is to use the A Dorian scale for a framework. Here, I'm adding passing notes to fill out the sequence, and I play the melody as a "six over four" cross-rhythmic line. To learn this, it's best to isolate each bar and play through it really slowly.

First, just learn the shape of the line in the first bar and work out a comfortable fingering. Don't worry about playing it in time. Once you have the sequence of notes under your fingers, then you can begin to think about the rhythms, still playing slowly. Practice to a metronome and after a while you'll get a feel for whether you're lagging behind or rushing to cram in the notes before the bar ends. Keep at it and you'll nail it.

Once you've worked on the individual bars, work on piecing them together. Refer to the audio throughout to capture the feel and phrasing.

Example 8e

Here's the full solo. There are some challenging passages in it so, again, isolate these and take them into your practice sessions to work on.

Example 8f – Full Solo

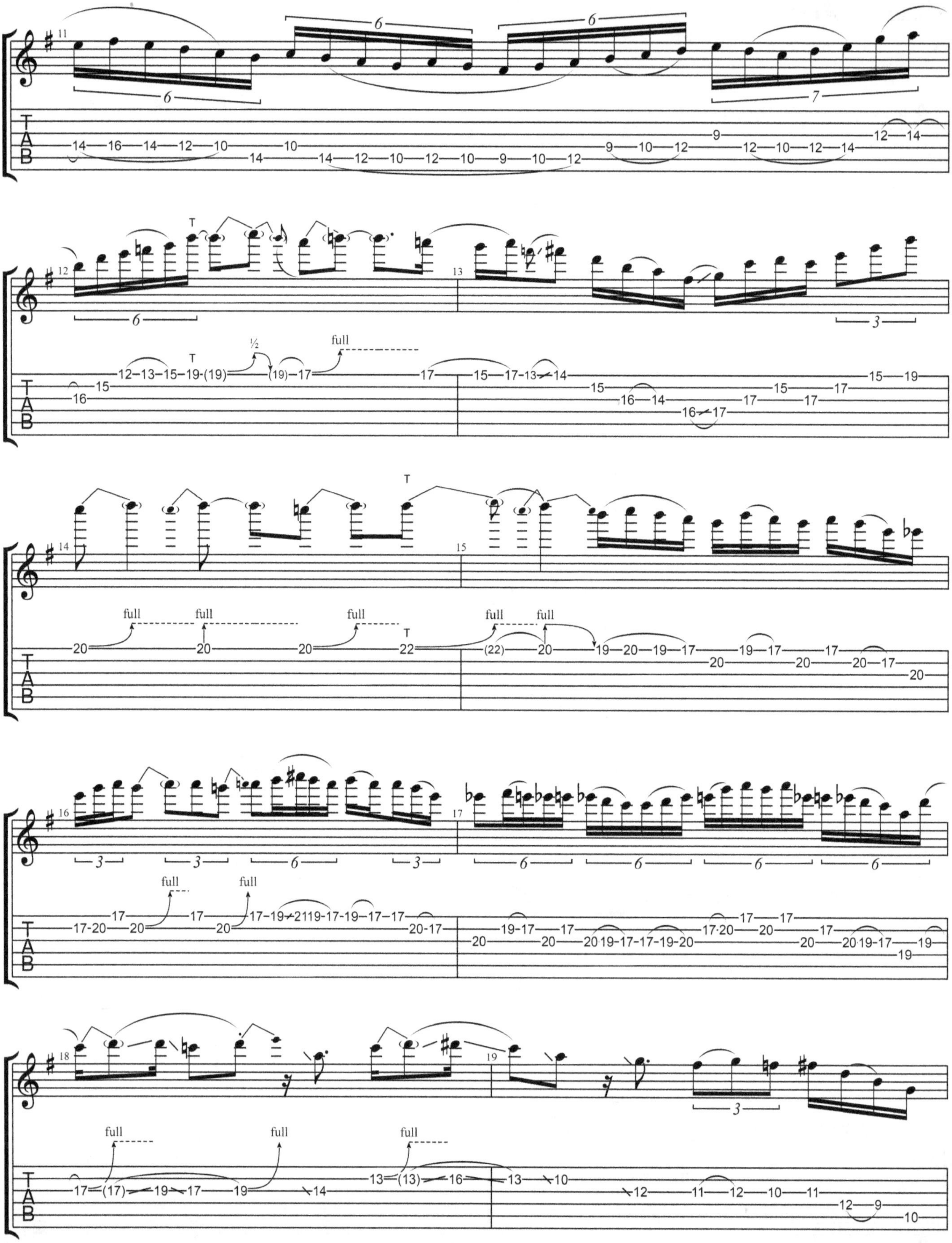
T
½
full
T
full
full
full
T
full
full
full
full
full
full
full

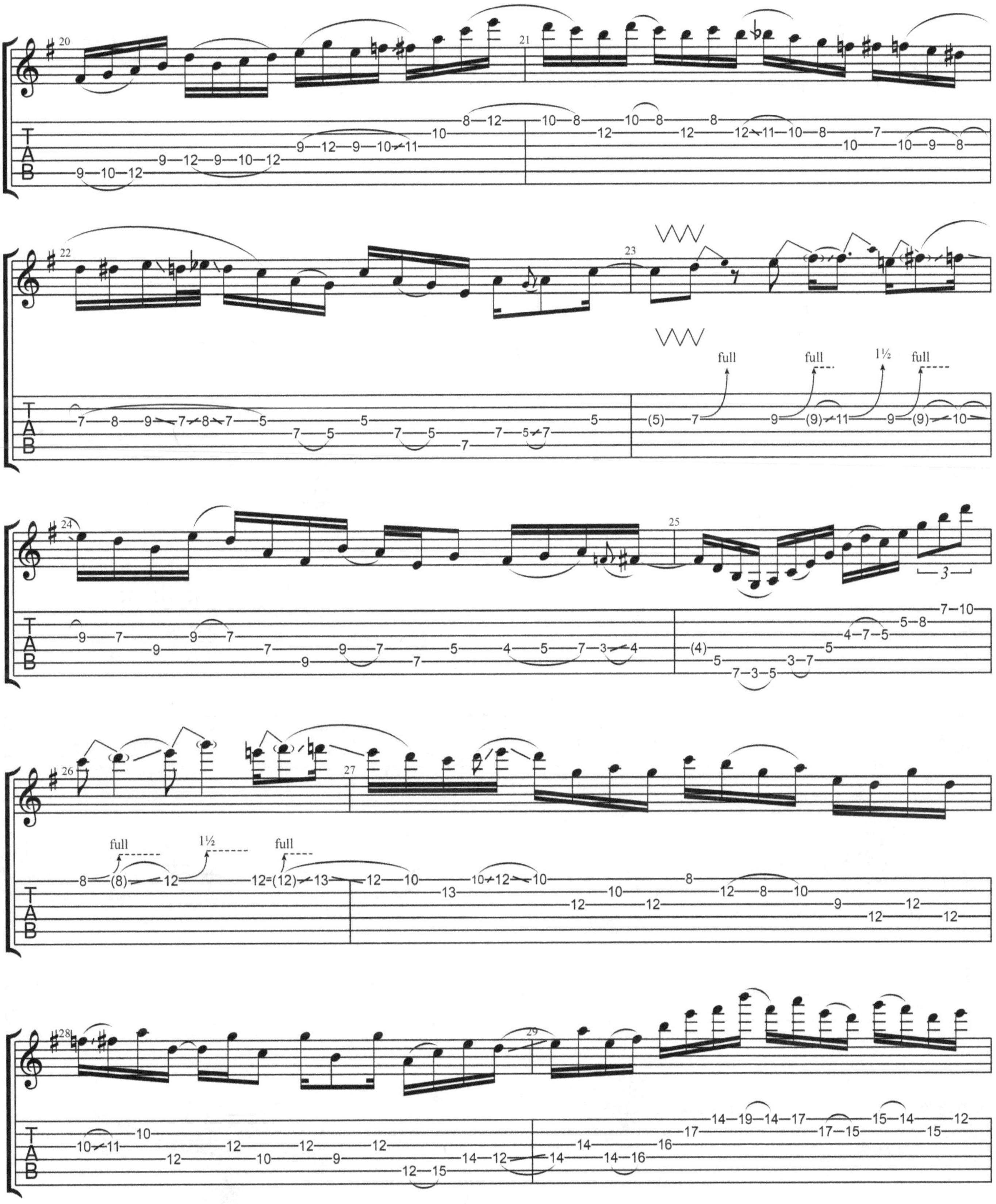
full
1½
TAB

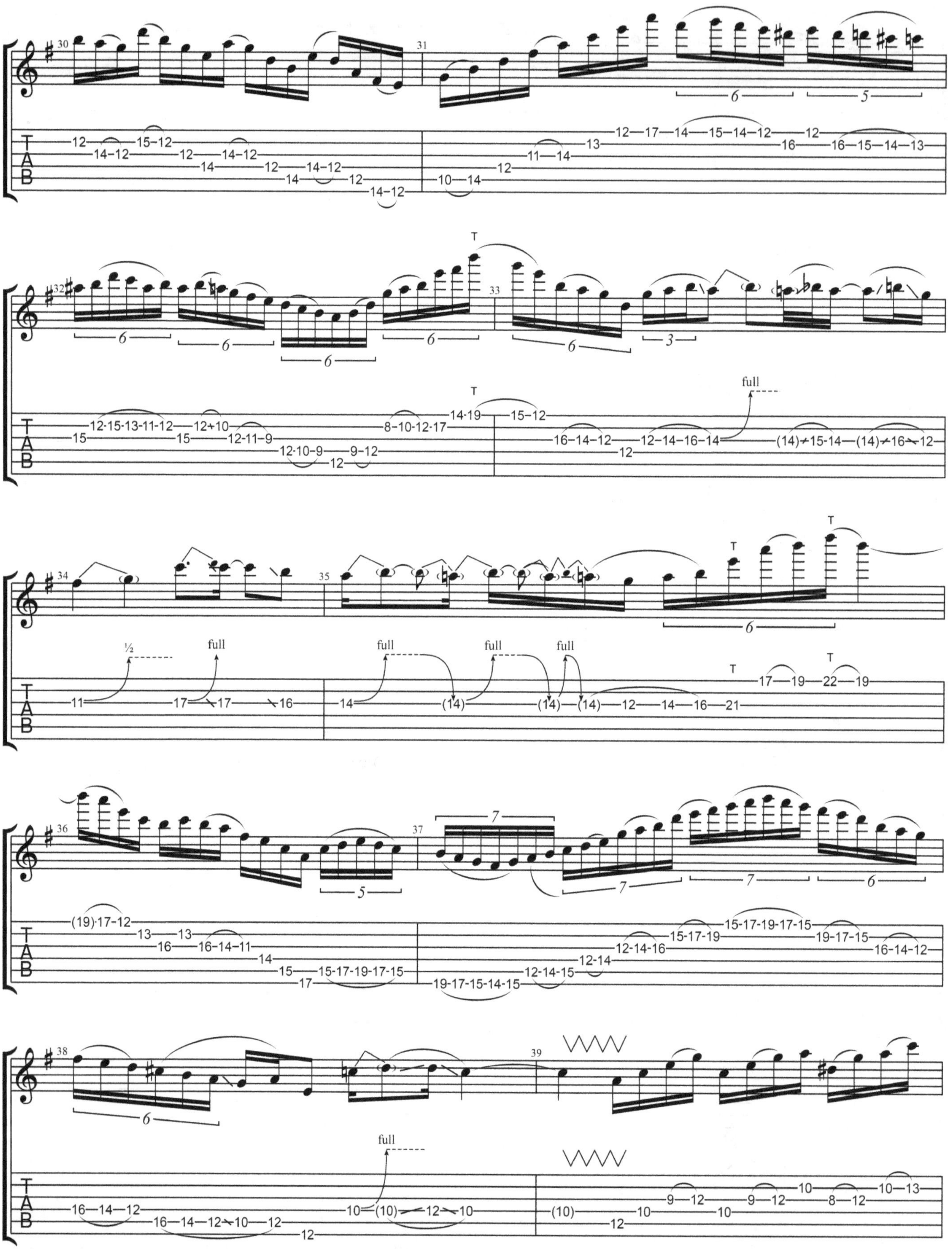
T
full
½
full
full
full
full
T
T
full

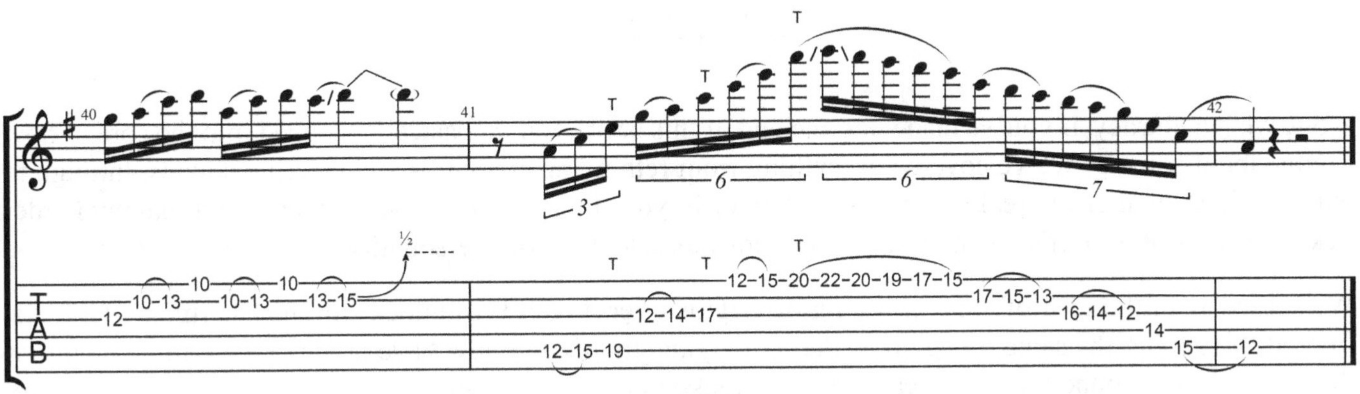

Conclusion

Wow, what a journey. If you've made it to the end of this book, you've basically stepped into the core of how I think about soloing. We've covered everything from rethinking arpeggios and layering sounds, through to phrasing ideas that create real movement and color in your lines. This has never been about playing harder licks for the sake of it. It's about giving your solos more depth, more personality, and more intention.

We started with the idea of superimposing arpeggios over a chord to unlock different harmonic textures. Instead of running the same arpeggio as the underlying chord, you now have a handful of creative options that immediately sound more musical. Then we looked at how to integrate my personal scale shapes, built around consistent fingering patterns, so you can move between scales and arpeggios without friction. From there, it was all about building lines that flow: ascending licks that hide the arpeggio inside scale movement, and descending ones that feel loose and expressive but still target the right notes.

As the chapters went on, we introduced more color. Chromatic passing tones, half-step approaches, little tweaks that let you push outside the key and then resolve back in. These things add tension and make your solos sound more interesting without having to overthink. But the big shift often comes when players start focusing on rhythm and phrasing. I always say that the right note at the wrong time is still the wrong note. So, we spent time disrupting the predictable, building phrasing ideas using simple intervals in new ways, and creating grooves and lines that move across the beat instead of sitting directly on top of it

Throughout this whole book, I wanted to give you tools that sound sophisticated but are surprisingly easy to apply once you've spent time with them. I hope you're now seeing how this system allows you to build a strong framework for your solos, while still being completely open to your own creativity.

So what now? First, experiment. Take the ideas from this book and apply them to other keys, other grooves, other genres. If you're playing over a major chord, try dropping in a IIIm7 or V7 arpeggio. Move your scale shapes around. Write new licks using the same fingering templates. Add hybrid picking or legato or whatever feels natural to you. That's how you find your voice. For me, I knew early on I wasn't going to be the fastest guy in the room, so I leaned into harmony and composition. I wanted the depth and phrasing of someone like George Benson, but with the energy of rock. You can build your own version of that too.

If you're looking for next steps, spend time just getting comfortable with these ideas. Play them over simple vamps. Build fluency before you go looking for more complexity. And when you're ready, start applying these concepts to progressions that change chords. You'll be amazed how quickly it sounds like you're outlining the harmony just by using smart arpeggio choices. Also, listen to other players. Transcribe solos. Pay attention to how other guitarists phrase, how they resolve tension, how they use rhythm. A bit of music theory can help too, especially if you're curious about melodic minor and other harmonic options.

But above all, have fun. If it's enjoyable, you'll do it more. If you do it more, you'll improve faster. This stuff only really sticks when you're using it to make music you love. Jam, record yourself, experiment. Over time, these tools will start to blend into your own style. That's when it gets exciting.

I hope this has been inspiring and useful. Keep asking questions, keep exploring sounds, and keep building your own voice. If something feels good under your fingers and sounds good to your ears, trust it. That's where the magic starts. Thanks for spending this time with me. I'll be rooting for you.

Have fun!

Greg